Dr. Gwilym Wyn Roberts
and Robert Workman

Positive ageing –
transitioning into
retirement and beyond.

An appreciative coaching approach for health
and social care professionals

novum ◢ pro

www.novum-publishing.co.uk

© 2019 novum publishing

ISBN 978-3-99064-564-2
Editing: B.Ed (Hons) Julie Hoyle
Cover photo:
Benjavisa Ruangvaree | Dreamstime.com
Cover design, layout & typesetting:
novum publishing

www.novum-publishing.co.uk

CONTENTS

Chapter 4 – Marital status, gender, sexual orientation, occupational engagement and retirement transition

"Aging, in the sense of becoming a whole person,
is not the same as growing old."

(Moore, p17)

FOREWORD

Assumptions about being old

My family members have been and continue to be amazing achievers in life, but also in retirement. One person is a professional singer, and though she does not perform any longer is still an active choir member and manages the soprano section. Another family member, a former professor and minister, has continued to study and research in libraries, attends every concert he can, and keeps up his lifelong journaling. Yet another, also a retired professor, continued to work in the academic setting well past her 70th birthday and still runs (years later) workshops for staff members at her retirement centre. Our eldest family member, though now very ill, continued with multiple book clubs, chaired the resident committee that supported employees of her retirement community, read two major newspapers every day, and served a couple of stints as her alumna sorority chapter president, all between ages 82 and 88 (Wilson 2009).

ABOUT THE AUTHORS

Dr Gwilym Wyn Roberts

EdD, MA, Diploma in Applied Psychosynthesis,
Diploma in the College of Occupational Therapists

Gwilym has worked in health and social care practice and education for over 30 years. He was Director of Occupational Therapy and Senior Lecturer at Cardiff University until 2016, when he retired from full-time paid employment at the age of 55. He has a Masters degree in Further and Higher Education from the Institute of Education in London and a Professional Doctorate from the School of Social Sciences at Cardiff University. His passion for research is in the areas of appreciative inquiry and positive psychology. He is particularly interested in ageing adults' experience relating to compassion and dignity and in 2015 co-authored a book entitled '*Appreciative Healthcare Practice – a guide to compassionate person-centred care*'. He works as a healthcare educational consultant and a retirement coach and now sits on the Wales Crown Prosecution Hate Modern Slavery and Human Trafficking Panel. Gwilym now embraces the time to also engage in a wide variety of creative and recreational occupations of choice.

Robert Workman

BSc (Hons) Occupational Therapy,
MSc Ageing Studies

Robert qualified as an Occupational Therapist in 2003, graduating from Cardiff University with a first class degree. In 2011 he gained a Masters degree in Ageing Studies from Swansea University. Throughout his career as an occupational therapist working for the NHS in his local hospitals, Robert has maintained a special interest in the role of meaningful activity in the development of the independence and well-being of ageing adults. His MSc research explored the role of meaningful activity in the retirement transition process. Whilst working as an Associate Lecturer at Cardiff University, Robert and Gwilym discovered a joint interest in this field. Robert is currently an occupational therapy manager employed by Abertawe Bro Morgannwg University Health Board in South Wales. He engages in a variety of meaningful activities and is already planning for his retirement in 20 years' time!

INTRODUCTION

> "Twenty years from now you will be more disappointed by the things you didn't do than by the one's you did do. So throw off the bowlines. Sail away from the safe harbor. Catch the trade winds in your sails. Explore. Dream. Discover."
> Mark Twain

Why write this book?

In writing this book, we aim to offer an alternative approach to that of having a purely negative perspective of ageing adults, to one of appreciation and affirmation. Please note that we refer to this population not as older adults but as ageing adults. We do this to avoid any potential stereotypical and negative attitude towards the word 'older'. This also encourages individuals to determine at what point do they consider themselves to be getting 'old', as 'ageing' for us is a more dynamic and affirmative term to progressing years of life. A more positive attitude is key to transitional retirement. Whilst fully recognising that we all may have anxieties and worries about retirement as a life stage, the purpose here is not to close but to open doors for change. Real time strategic change of this kind brings together a recognising of patterns from the past with an aspiration for a more positive future, creating a commitment to what we will do differently in order to plan to get there. The focus is on current reality as the basis for planning and change, and the opportunity to mine the wisdom of individuals to move on successfully, now and in the future. We aim to encourage a bridging of 'both/and', rather than a split of an 'either/or' approach, in order to harness what is working now in the design for the future. To achieve this direction, the work advocates the underlying principles of appreciative inquiry and positive psychology. We will explore the ways in which these collectively inform how the individual and people in general approach and view ageing and transitional retirement. Essentially, appreciative inquiry is based on the premise that all aspects of our lives and the systems in which we are employed, work well to some degree. It is the individual's role to uncover where and how those systems are working to their advantage; to focus energy and attention on understanding why and how these work; and seek support to build on those conditions that foster positivity and well-being. This journey though often thought to be isolating, does not have to be so. We encourage that one dialogues with fellow retirees whatever their age, and access those professionals who may have expert knowledge and skills to apply some coaching skills as a way to guide and support the transitional process. In this context coaching is a dynamic partnership between coach (healthcare professional) and client (ageing adult). The coach's role is to create a supportive relationship built on trust and confidentiality. In transitional retirement, an opportunity exists to give individuals and groups the opportunity to identify personal strengths, aspirations and concerns. Effective coaching guides the ageing adult to gain insight into their values, beliefs, behaviour and motivation, therefore, potentially raising self-awareness and self-worth. Through effectively applying some coaching skills, a retirement coach can support the ageing adult to make confident retirement decisions in order to embrace the future with security and confidence.

Occupational science may be a useful approach in this context as it could be a way to better understand human time use. In the first paper on the topic in the late 90s, it was proposed that: "occupational science is the study of the human as an occupational being including the need for and capacity to engage in and orchestrate daily occupations and work in the environment over the lifespan" (Yerxa et al 1998, p6). Occupational scientists as a result, have long recognised the correlation between activity, health and well-being and the literature surrounding health and activity is prolific. However, the attention to why people choose certain occupations at retirement, as opposed to others, is rarely addressed. For instance, is merely being active enough to enhance the transition into retirement and increase the chance of successful ageing? Or is there a connection when transitioning into retirement between occupational choice, health and well-being? With this in mind, we recognise at this point that is it very difficult to acknowledge all cultural aspects of ageing and retirement, and therefore we invite the reader to interpret the content of this book in relation to their own cultural values, beliefs, traditions and norms – we stress the importance of this in the hope that recognising rich cultural differences will be the foundation for deep reflections and learning.

Why is this book needed?

This book is unique in two ways. Firstly, it offers an insightful and practical guide to a variety of healthcare professionals working with ageing adults, as well as to human resource personnel. Equally important, this book may be utilised as a self-help resource to those individuals who are either planning for, or experiencing the transition into retirement and beyond. Secondly, it commits to seeing ageing and the process of transitional retirement from a more appreciative and affirmative perspective. It invites healthcare professionals to consider continuous professional development in the field of coaching as a way to empower and guide ageing adults towards and into transitional retirement and beyond. This book advocates the development and application of skills and knowledge that will equip such health and social care professionals and others to extend their scope of practice to this new and exciting emerging arena of coaching – in this context as a general coach for ageing adults and in particular in the more specific area of retirement coaching.

Both authors' vast experience as health and social care professionals working with ageing adults offers a level of expertise in offering a well-researched evidence base and reflective models of practice. Weaving real life examples of individuals going through transitional retirement offers valuable pause points, where the reader is invited to reflect, learn and apply new skills and knowledge. The book offers a practical guide and suggests new and innovative models in addition to theoretically and empirically derived frameworks to assist effective support and professional intervention. In applying this work in practice, the possibility emerges that those who we might judge to be most limited and, at worst, burdensome, may hold a vital capacity and capability for organisations and communities whilst finding a sense of fulfilment through chosen occupation.

Who is this book for?

This book is aimed at every person who has either a professional and/ or personal interest in how ageing is perceived in society and in particular, understanding how ageing adults make the most successful transition into retirement and beyond. Its main objective is for it to be used as both a practical guide and a reference resource for a variety of people including health and social care professionals, a spectrum of health and social care students, and any individual aspiring to become or currently practising as a retirement coach. We also hope that this book will be a useful resource to those who are often ignored or misunderstood, those very individuals who are actually facing or entering full or part time retirement and who may wish to more fully understand the dynamics of this important transitional period and life event.

This book is driven by the professional experience of both authors and an unwavering shared interest in this field, in addition to research evidence realised from their post- graduate level studies and professional practice in the private and public sector. As the authors, we feel strongly that there is a need for an alternative and more innovative and practical approach to working with and supporting ageing adults, especially through the retirement transition stage. One author is in the transitional period of his retirement, and the second practices as a manager and senior occupational therapist with specialist knowledge and research interest in working with ageing adults.

When considering research evidence there seems to have been a growth in the literature on positive ageing. This said, it is felt that there is room for more published text that focusses specifically on how appreciative inquiry can potentially foster a more positive approach to working with ageing adults during this life stage. There appears to be a culture change within healthcare education and practice where allied health professionals (AHPs) and other medical professionals, such as nurses and social workers, could consciously encourage and support ageing adults to maintain more choice, independence and well-being. Such support is now being increasingly integrated into services offered by a growing band of such professionals. We propose that acquiring the required coaching skills through continuous professional development will encourage health and social care professionals to become health and retirement coaches. As such, the scope of professional practice is broadening, in particular in relation to the need to improve and change behaviour, attitude, quality of support and support offered to an ageing adult. In response, themes and ideas presented in this book will contribute toward the enhancement of professional health and retirement coaching skills and practice as a way to enhance the quality of support offered to ageing adults. The aim is also to provide insight on such matters to other sector services within public, voluntary and private industry, those whose skills lie in human resources and who routinely deal effectively (or not) with personnel who are moving towards the transition into retirement. Finally, let's not forget the most important community of all, those ageing adults themselves who may benefit from this book as they prepare, plan and seek whatever support is appropriate for them during this important, and exciting life stage.

This book will specifically offer a developmental, practical and educational guide for professionals, health and social care students and all those involved in learning about how to enable successful transition to retirement. Research evidence and case studies will be presented to underpin the development of an appreciative approach as a way to enhance behaviours and attitudes toward ageing. This will be further underpinned by key theories, current and historical legislative and policy influences. Pause points will offer time for reflection as a way to engage with, and illustrate, key themes. Some reflective questions are asked as a way to encourage individuals to record their learning and consider key issues that have been raised. Such tasks will be invaluable to those professionals who need to maintain their continuing professional development (CPD).

What this book aims to achieve

The book clearly aims to encourage every reader to appreciate a more positive perspective of the experiences of ageing, as a way to fully understand the ways in which ageing adults view and prepare for transitional retirement and beyond. It is important to develop a more positive (appreciative) outlook, acknowledging that some aspects of society, and indeed the media, continue to hold some stereotypical negative perceptions of what it means to grow old. This book also challenges the reader to question at what age individuals are categorised as being old!

We sincerely hope that this book will also be of value to those individuals facing, or who have already entered, this transitional period, those individuals who are themselves considering or are fully engaged in the health and well-being retirement transition process. This book aims to offer some useful guidance and a deeper, much more appreciative, affirmative and positive understanding of their experience.

Historically and cross culturally, the practice of retirement may be anything but common. The demographic forces of decreased mortality, better health care systems, and increased longevity have contributed to larger numbers of ageing adults than ever before in our history. Too often ageing adults, who have been successful and productive individuals, are at times trivialised in their everyday lives and interactions. At times, this occurs unintentionally because of unconscious assumptions about people who are growing old. To suggest that culture plays an important role in such decisions about transitions from labour force participation to retirement seems reasonable. Sociologists and anthropologists have long focussed on culture as a determinant of human behaviour and have noted a strong inclination of individuals to conform to certain norms, to behave in ways similar to their fellow citizens. Of central importance is the recognition that cultural factors will influence all discussions about ageing adults and the transitional journey into retirement. As such, no assumptions about any specific culture or society have been made within this book.

How is this book structured?

Chapter 1 defines ageing and explores the opportunities and challenges of an ageing population. It will guide individuals on how they may engage in a more positive approach to ageing and retirement with consideration given to a number of recognised activity-focussed theories on ageing. This chapter will also reflect on some established and, at times, stereotypical attitudes and behaviours to this life stage, with relation to chosen theories e.g. positive psychology and appreciative inquiry. Some current and historical polices and legislation will be analysed and considered.

Chapter 2 argues that improvements in retirement transition can be more easily attained by building on perceptions of success, rather than focussing on failure. It is also suggested that positive aspects of our relationships with others and ourselves should be a starting point from which we can find a way forward. Based on these principles, appreciative inquiry and the 4 D Model are discussed. This is a recognised model of 'intervention' and research that encourages affirmative action, behaviour and organisational development will be explored. Practical issues will be identified and discussed, for example, ethics, individual and team factors. This chapter will include suggestions on how appreciative inquiry can be introduced as a way to enhance personal and professional development and positively influence behaviours and personal approaches to ageing adults and retirement.

Chapter 3 aims to highlight the key issues raised within the literature on activity and occupations in later life. It will describe the nature of the ageing population and discuss a number of theories of ageing, such as structured dependency, disengagement theory, activity theory and continuity theory. Active ageing strategies will then be introduced with reference to international and local initiatives.

Chapter 4 examines the issues faced by individuals during the retirement transition process, including the impact of gender, culture, marital status and engagement in meaningful activities. This chapter will also look at adversity, and the need for resilience and transformational growth towards retirement and beyond.

Chapter 5 introduces the concept of mindfulness and explores how this can be used to facilitate creative, independent lifestyle redesign in preparation for and following retirement. This chapter will look at the growing evidence that mindfulness is effective in lowering levels of psychological distress and elevating levels of well-being and life satisfaction. It will again challenge stereotypes and presumptions about ageing adults and their ability to effect change independently.

Chapter 6 provides specific guidance on how appreciative inquiry as a technique motivates and empowers stakeholders (all those who may work in the field or benefit from their professional support and intervention) to change their life, situation and organisation. This chapter will guide key stakeholders in how to embrace and promote a more respectful, compassionate and dignified approach to ageing and retirement. For these reasons, appreciative inquiry can become the chosen means of enhancing and affirming quality of life and well-being for professionals and stakeholders. By encouraging openness and negotiation among stakeholders in this context, this methodology supports attempts to give collective and organisation-wide ownership and authorship of positive transformation. It provides a procedure in which reflection becomes a collaborative means of improving systems and is negotiated, not imposed, due to its person-centred focus. Therefore, consequent changes are more likely to be accepted by individuals since they have been proactive in evaluating themselves and their aspirations for a satisfying older age.

Chapter 7 explores the value of developing a person-centred retirement coaching approach for those individuals challenged by the retirement process. Coaching focusses on the occupation of the health and social care worker as an aspirational health and retirement coach. The ability to coach is increasingly employed in professional practice in leisure, health and social care. This will show how creativity, intuition, imagination and integrity can emerge together with qualities such as compassion and dignity to inform the coaching skills of the health and retirement coach. The chapter presents how advancing coaching capability is the key to modelling respect, compassion and dignity in later life. An innovative model of practice is described as a way to guide retirement coaches to achieve effective intervention with ageing adults. The 3 Eye Model highlights the sensitive balance for health and retirement coaches to view ageing adults through different lenses and perspectives that are analytical, appreciative and creative. This will describe how a coaching relationship may offer a meaningful channel through which individuals, groups and organisations are able to develop and sustain change. This chapter will provide an insight into how those professionals can build confidence and expertise to coach and apply this to enable ageing adults to transition effectively into retirement.

Chapter 8 offers a summary and a reflection on the key points raised in the book. In summary, each chapter will build on offering an appreciation of how to:

Apply a more affirmative and more appreciative approach to ageing and retirement with consideration given to a number of recognised activity-focussed ageing theories.

Gain a deeper understanding of the health benefits and the role of meaningful occupations in the retirement transition process, including activity choice and perceived benefits.

Gain insight into the impact of factors such as gender and marital status on successful retirement transition.

Promote a more creative approach to potential inactivity and the negative consequences on health and well-being.

Explore the benefits of mindfulness and its role in active ageing.

Explore the role of the professional as a health and retirement coach, and to offer effective professional support, guide and intervention to enable successful retirement transition.

Offer a coaching skill base for professionals and retirement coaches to maximise on the available support and guidance available for ageing adults.

Why the focus on transitional retirement and beyond?

Retirement is a term which defines the experience of an individual leaving his or her main career, but in reality it can cover a range of scenarios including: leaving full-time work for good for family care, recreation, leisure, part time employment, engaging in voluntary work or even embarking on opportunities for self-employment. Due to an ageing population it is estimated that by 2050, one in three people worldwide will be aged 60 and above (United Nations 2010). Retirement is a life stage experienced by most individuals at some stage, the transition into which ideally requires the restructuring of daily routines and social contacts and a reframing of anxieties into affirmative action.

In modern society it is thought that a large proportion of the life course becomes devoted to succeeding within the workplace and increasing one's social life, but in reality very few people plan for their retirement transition and decide what they will do once they have retired. This historical pattern, however, is changing for an increasing number of younger people who, unlike previous generations, appear to be in a much clearer and much more positive personal (and financial) situation to actually realise an earlier than expected transitional retirement.

Most would like to believe that retirement is one of the most important occupational transitions, where some of the main focus is on rebuilding one's occupational identity and engaging with more freedom and creativity to pursue activities that we refer to in this book as 'occupation of choice'. Attitudes to such engagement in activities following retirement have changed drastically since the middle of the last century.

According to research undertaken by jobs website, Monster (2015), people hit their earning peak at the age of 50 and start looking forward to retirement just five years later at 55. The study, in which those who had just entered retirement were questioned, found that the average Briton is employed by six companies during their working life and most change career paths twice. One in ten (10%) remained for ten or more years in the same job without being promoted. When reflecting on their careers, the study revealed the biggest regrets held by those who had just retired. A fifth (20%), wished they had not got so stressed out and worked up about their work; one in seven, (14%), regretted not leaving their work earlier every day as they had wished that they had not worked longer hours than needed. Meanwhile, 13% regretted not pushing themselves further, similarly 13% wished they had not stayed in a career that was not right for them and 8% expressed a desire to retire earlier. Attitudes do appear to be changing, but far too often people experience a predominantly negative response to this transitional period, with many, including the media, making dire assumptions in relation to quality of life, purpose in life and the individual's actual choice to retire, and at the age one chooses to do so.

A personal context

Health and social care professionals, occupational therapists in particular, have a deep and specialist interest in the topic of meaningful activity. The authors' personal interests in the topic stems from their own endeavours for transitional retirement, in addition to their own observation of the way some friends, colleagues and indeed parents approached and adapted to life following retirement. In reflecting on his own parents, one of the authors observed his mother and father who had been in employment throughout their adulthood, both working full-time for several decades prior to retirement at 65 years of age. However, as retirement loomed, he noticed that his parents approached this life change in very different ways, both in a practical and an emotional sense. While his father spoke of excitement at the anticipation of having more time to indulge in hobbies and spend with grandchildren, his mother expressed anxiety about the risk of becoming bored and depressed without formal employment to fill her days. As a result, the planning that both parents made for their retirement was very different. Further discussions affirmed that the transition into retirement can be a complex issue for many ageing adults, difficult but also potentially exciting, affirmative and life changing.

A professional context

Those professionals who consider themselves to be occupational scientists find meaningful activity in retirement professionally engaging. The foundation of the occupational therapy profession, for example, is a belief that every individual needs to participate in purposeful activity to maintain physical and psychological well-being. In both professional and personal lives, it has become apparent that continued engagement in activity is a high priority for most people following retirement and all of us need to give much thought to how this can be achieved. The changing activity patterns of people as they age, and following retirement, has been studied more since the middle of the last century. A literature search revealed a plethora of research carried out by a number of disciplines, including occupational therapists and gerontologists, that related to the issue of activity in later life and retirement (Hewitt, Howie and Feldman 2010; Katz 2000; Ball, Corr, Knight and Lowis 2007; Nimrod 2008), but arguably more is needed. Over the next 50 years, the United Kingdom and the rest of the developed world will continue to experience an unprecedented change in the fabric of society. As life expectancy increases and the birth rate remains low, the proportion of the population growing old is increasing dramatically (World Health Organisation (WHO) 2002, United Nations (UN) 2010). An ageing society is far too often and wrongly seen negatively solely in terms of increasing dependency, and almost as a burden! But in reality, as ageing adults become an ever more significant proportion of the population, society will increasingly depend upon the contribution they make to the economy, society and the future of purposeful and meaningful occupation.

For most ageing adults, retirement is an important milestone that is associated with changes in daily routines, social roles, contacts, income and self-esteem. Engagement in meaningful occupations has a key role in retirement transition and it is argued that most of us will choose only to live as long as there is a purpose for life within our psyche. Therefore, if the population is ageing, and resisting what it means to be ageing, there is an implied question about what we do not yet understand or acknowledge about the 'meaning' of ageing. Today's ageing adults are already challenging old preconceptions. In the main they are healthier; they are making an economic contribution; they are breaking with the notion that old age and poverty are synonymous and ageing adults are no longer more likely to be poor than younger people; and there is a significant dependency on ageing adults to sustain the voluntary or unpaid work sector of our society, in addition to family support, through child minding occupations. Many ageing adults are already enjoying life to the full, making the most of the opportunities of age and making a huge contribution to their families, communities and society in general. However, as the numbers of ageing adults grow, society faces challenges too. One challenge is to unlock the potential for ageing adults to play an even greater role, in particular when considering the future of occupation. A second is to enable society to appreciate and prepare more effectively for new and positive challenges in later life.

The early part of the 21st century certainly did see progress in combating inequality and social injustice in old age, particularly when considering employment and work. Some would argue that equality of opportunity inspires individuals to fulfil their potential in relation to creativity, occupation and work (Wilcock 2001). However, whilst most equality legislation is meant to protect and promote equality for all, many believe the law falls short of doing so as far as age is concerned. The setting up of the Single Equality Body in 2004 did, to a large extent, embed in all policies directed towards ageing adults the values of active independence, quality, choice, occupation and work that had been championed in other areas. The role of engaging in activity in later life has been identified by a number of international organisations and incorporated into guidance for use by world governments (WHO 2002; UN 1992). Such guidance are important for policy makers in the United Kingdom, and as an example they were included in the National Service Framework for Older People in Wales, a document that "sets national standards designed to ensure that as we grow older we are enabled to maintain our health, well-being and independence for as long as possible" (Welsh Assembly Government 2006 pp. 6–7).

In the context of family life, organisational work, management, entrepreneurship, and within an active global environment in which competition is service based and knowledge intensive, there appear to be new opportunities for ageing adults to use applied knowledge, initiative, and their creative energies in a wide range of occupations, including those working for small companies or in self-employment. For example, some organisations such as B & Q in the United Kingdom, because of life and social experience are increasingly likely to employ individuals over 60, a trend that appears to be growing. In addition, some of the main voluntary and charity organisations appear to recognise that maturity, human creativity and individual initiative are far more important as a source of competitive advantage than homogeneity and conformity. More companies are expected to hire ageing adults with new laws on anti-age discrimination and retirement in place. Changes to tax laws will also mean that workers do not have to retire before receiving their pension.

Research shows that adults want the choice and the Government need to be seen to more effectively advocate that ageing adults have been encouraged to return to work. The challenge is not to force employees to fit the corporate model of the 'organisational man or woman', but to build organisations flexible enough to exploit the idiosyncratic knowledge and unique skills offered by each individual employee and in particular those deemed to be ageing and more experienced in work and life.

Professionals as retirement coaches – coaching ageing adults facing changes in life

Working with ageing adults in transitional retirement and beyond is one approach to coaching in which health and social care professionals may choose to specialise. It is important to stress again that coaching is increasingly becoming an accredited profession, with an emphasis on a continual deepening of coaching competencies. The same will apply to some counsellors and complimentary therapists, although their titles may not be protected by law in the same way as allied health professionals and most health and social care professions, and they may well not be regulated in the same way. This said, general coaching skills can be utilised by a wide variety of health and social care workers and others who are in a supporting role of ageing adults.

When establishing a coaching relationship with an ageing adult the process aims to address specific personal projects, successes, general conditions and transitions in the person's life, relationships or occupations of choice. In transitional retirement terms, a person-centred coach will explore opportunities to examine with the individual what may be going on in the moment, discovering what visible or hidden obstacles or challenges might be in place, and facilitating a course of action to permit life to be what the individual wants it to be. Historically, there has been more interest shown in offering financial preparation and planning, and although this remains a key focus for most ageing adults, further focus has emerged lately on ensuring psychological, emotional and practical support.

The next chapter will define ageing and explore the opportunities and challenges of an ageing population.

CHAPTER 1

AGEING AND RETIREMENT

"Retirement, a time to do what you want to do, when you want to do it,
where you want to do it, and, how you want to do it."
Catherine Pulsifer

This chapter will offer a guide on how society may engage with a more positive and appreciative approach to ageing and retirement by considering a number of recognised activity-focussed theories of ageing and some important literature in the field. This chapter will also reflect on established and, at times, stereotypical attitudes and behaviours to this life stage. Important current and historical polices and legislation will be considered.

Retirement

Retirement is a term which defines the experience of an individual leaving his or her main career, but in reality it can cover a range of scenarios including: leaving full-time work for a vision to pursue leisurely activities such as sport and travel, a caring role, part-time employment, voluntary work or even for ambitions for self-employment. Retirement is a life stage which requires the restructuring of daily routines and social contacts. With a large proportion of the life course devoted to succeeding within the workplace and increasing one's family and social life, more young people appear to be planning for their retirement transition by deciding what they will do once that opportunity is taken, and increasingly so at a much earlier time in their lives.

Retirement can be one of the most important occupational transitions, where the main focus is on rebuilding occupational identity (Kielhofner 2008). Individuals may need to more fully embrace occupational engagement, plan how they may spend their time and identify the type of support and positive vision they might require.

Historically, the occupational transition into retirement has been explored by many researchers from across the world. Jonsson, Borell and Sadlo in (2000), for example, interviewed 12 Swedish participants as part of a longitudinal study over a seven-year period. Findings highlighted that some participants managed a transition into a satisfying pattern of retirement, whereas others found it an ongoing process of frustration and dissatisfaction. As times have changed in both attitude and legislation, further research in relation to the retirement transition in other cultures may be required. Pettican and Prior (2011) also conducted a qualitative study with eight British participants, exploring occupational transition into retirement. Findings highlighted that there was a close relationship between participant's engagement in occupation following retirement and their perceived health and well-being.

Attitudes to engagement in activities following retirement have changed drastically since the middle of the last century. The introduction of mandatory retirement by the National Insurance Act 1946, for example, allowed ageing adults to finish work at defined ages (60 for women and 65 for men), but this was not always viewed as a positive transition due to the negative effects that were thought to accompany ending employment. In the following decades, as life expectancy increased and ageing adults exhibited enhanced health and quality of life into older age, retirement came to be viewed as a period in which people could enjoy their lives without the need for employment (Harper 2006 pp. 100–101). However, the transition to this stage of life still remains challenging for a vast number of people and for a wide variety of reasons.

Activity, occupation and retirement transition

The transition into retirement has to be viewed as a significant period in an individual's life and it is proposed that careers and paid full/part-time employment does, to a degree, fulfil a basic human need to utilise skills, apply knowledge, occupy time, develop social relationships, enhance self-image, develop identity, and establish status within society. Some may feel that retirement has a significant impact on daily routines, social support, relationships, roles, self–esteem and use of time, but this cannot be true of all perspectives. A growing number of individuals believe the opposite, that retirement gives freedom, creativity, positive changes to routines, enhanced social support, improved relationships, develops different roles, boosts self– esteem and maximises on the use of time. This affirmative and appreciative perspective during this life stage may enhance a much healthier life journey by boosting the well-being agenda, building on leisure, recreational and occupational activities and work. A more positive attitude and appreciative approach can potentially guide and support a much more personally acceptable occupational balance in all aspects of life.

The impact of retirement on engagement in activity is acknowledged by a variety of ageing theories that will be explored further in Chapter 3. Concisely, while Disengagement Theory marks it as a time when individuals begin to withdraw from activity, Activity Theory suggests that this begins a process of increased activity, and Structured Dependency Theory labels it as a process that is often enforced and may signal a period of reduced income and restricted opportunities. However, more positively, Continuity Theory reflects that retirement may not be such a difficult transition if values and self-esteem are maintained through continued activity patterns.

In research terms, various studies consider different aspects of retirement. While some describe the economic perspective (Price and Balaswamy 2009; Kim 2009; Dew and Yorgason 2010; Shuey 2004; Gran 2008), others focus on preferred retirement age (Parry & Taylor 2007; Cebulla, Butt and Lyon 2007; Soidre 2005; Brougham and Walsh 2009). Other studies acknowledge the influence that factors such as planning (Ogunbameru and Asa 2008; Hewitt, Howie and Feldman 2010) or gender and marital status have on experiences of retirement (Barnes and Parry 2004; Davey and Szinovacz 2004; Kim and Moen 2001; Kulik 2001; Kulik 2002; Pienta 2003). There are also many research papers that address the use of activity in the lives of retired people (Litwin and Shiovitz-Ezra 2006; Pushkar et al 2010; Nimrod 2008; Everard 1999; Katz 2000; McMunn et al 2009; Agahi and Parker 2005; Gagliardi et al 2007), reflecting the wide range of approaches to this topic.

Victor (2005) and Reynolds (2009) described activity following retirement as filling an occupational role that employment fulfilled, and that "role losses in retirement need to be compensated for by the substitution of compensatory activities" (p.24).This is supported by Stewart (2005) who reports that after a 40-year career she then took time caring for her mother full-time. Such an adoption of new activities following retirement suggests the influence of Activity Theory. However Nimrod (2008) describes this 're-invention of self' by engagement in new activities as 'Innovation Theory'. The study suggests that individuals generally continue with previous activities following retirement, as more free time allows, and begin new activities over the duration of the retirement period. Such continuity in activity can clearly be related to Continuity Theory and, similarly, it is argued that adoption of new activities as individuals age may be due to adaptation to their changing needs to maintain continuity in identify and lifestyle, rather than promoting reinvention as Nimrod (2008) suggests. This once again reflects Continuity Theory and supports previously cited studies that activity engagement enhances well-being.

Due to an ageing population (United Kingdom, National Statistics 2010), it is estimated that by 2050, one in three people worldwide will be aged 60 and above (United Nations 2010). As a result, society will potentially witness the increasing age at which people retire (Pettican and Prior 2011). Indeed, retirement is a life stage that may be experienced by many people, and it may require the restructuring of daily routines and social contacts. Some individuals may decide what they may do once they have retired although this trend may well be changing with people investing more time into planning. If planning is to be effective, then more guidance and support to better plan and prepare for it may be required from professionals such as health and retirement coaches. Such investment may mean that individuals and support systems need to prepare psychologically, physically, emotionally, spiritually and in particular, in practical terms.

The benefits of planning post-retirement activity have been recognised by Hewitt, Howie, and Feldman (2010). Their study explored the pre-retirement planning of retired people in Australia. It was found that such variables as financial resources, social environments and personal experience influenced activity planning. This once again illustrates the relationship of structural and life course influences in retirement experiences and the transition process. The study suggests that all participants who were involved in pre-retirement planning "expressed an overall positive experience of retirement" (p. 14), potentially beneficial in optimising life satisfaction and well-being in older age.

Pause point – case study

Celia is due to retire in six months. She has been planning for retirement for a number of years and has reduced to part-time hours in work to help her adjust to a different daily routine. However, Celia has now become concerned that she will struggle to fill her extra spare time. In preparation for this, Celia has enrolled in several classes at her local college, she has joined a gym and she is considering becoming a dog owner.

What do you think are the benefits of Celia's pre-retirement planning?

Do you have any concerns about Celia's plans? If so, what are they?

If Celia was a friend or colleague, what would be your advice to her at this stage?

Record your thoughts and reflect what could be done differently if you were Celia, in addition to what support and guidance you would give her if you were working with her on transitional retirement.

Within any transitional period as defined and experienced by the individual person, the potential change in personal priorities as occurring during this period is important. Some ageing adults may engage in increased preoccupation with introspection, reflection and self-evaluation, particularly when relating to their occupations and past work. Others may be dealing with some existential questioning of the self, values, and life itself and in particular when related to personal achievement and success and what may follow post-employment. In practical terms it is about taking stock, a seeing of oneself in realistic terms. Depression/low mood may at times result because of shortfalls, disappointments, loss of role, redundancy and the prospect of retirement, but why must this negativity be the focus at this time? Some will have to deal with other people's negative projections, anxiety and fear with their own preconceived ideas of what retirement looks like. Such beliefs are at times driven by the media's obsession with making growing old seem bad. However, most people we suspect will have a vast array of overriding and affirmative plans for the future, post full-time employment. A positive perspective and an affirmative belief in ageing being a constructive and creative period can result in a more appreciative outlook by the self and others on the individual's transition into retirement and beyond.

Perspectives on ageing

There is no doubt that the developed world continues to experience an unprecedented change in the fabric of society. As life expectancy increases and the birth rate remains low, the proportion of the population growing old is increasing dramatically. An ageing society is too often wrongly seen solely in terms of increasing dependency. But in reality, as ageing adults become an ever more significant proportion of the population, society may increasingly become more dependent upon the contribution they can make to the economy and the future of occupation. This said, it appears that there are sectors where there remains a deep resistance to ageing, and the glorification and even worshipping of what it means to be young. This often manifests itself in a fascination with changing and perfecting personal appearance, and an acknowledgement that society at times discriminates against 'age', that we are 'ageist' in many ways, including in our organisational, occupational, leisure, working and sexual lives.

Whilst focussing on work as just one area, some may well believe that redundancy, unemployment or even early retirement can lead to a deterioration in an individual's psychological and physical state of health. This could be due to the high value placed on the younger worker. Yet at the same time, our lifespan is increasing, and society aspires to continue to extend the lifespan via medical technology and developments. But do we all want to be 'young' and live longer and yet have no wish to be 'old'?

This said, ageing adults have already begun to challenge old preconceptions. As far back as 2005, for example, Age Concern found that in general, ageing adults:

- were healthier;
- were making an economic contribution;
- were breaking with the notion that old age and poverty are synonymous and ageing adults are no longer any more likely to be poor than younger people.

Of significance is the fact that Age Concern also highlighted the increasing dependency on ageing adults to sustain the voluntary or unpaid work sector of society.

To truly understand the issues of an ageing population it may be necessary to decide at what age an individual is defined as old. This is no simple task as old age is not so easily reduced to a number. For example, when designing policy for the ageing population, The Welsh Assembly Government (WAG) considered the transition to old age began for some people at age 50, as it recognises that, "chronological age may not necessarily be a good guide to people's needs and concerns … (as) ageing adults are not a homogeneous group" (WAG 2007 p.5). However, Harper (2006) explains, "Demographically, age 60 or 65 is taken to represent old age" (p.3), while the World Health Organisation (2004) and the United Nations (2010 p.2) cite the age of 60 when describing the ageing population.

Pause point

Is old age related to the number of years a person has been alive?

How do YOU define old age for yourself and for others in your life? What may be the influencing factors, if any?

Do you agree with the age statements above? If not, what counter argument could you present?

Reflect on your own perceptions, and what factors may influence your thoughts. It may be useful to think about family and friends who may be ageing adults. How fulfilled are their lives and what are the main influencing factors?

Inequalities and perceptions

Successfully dealing with demographic change may mean shedding outdated stereotypical mindsets about retirement and the process of ageing. Debate about demographic change too often focuses on financial issues, extra costs on the state, health/social care, and changes in the 'dependency ratio'. It is true that these future costs may well pose real challenges to the welfare state, and raise questions about the extent to which it is right for one generation to commit their successors. Without doubt, these challenges have to be addressed by modern day society. However, they should not dominate society's thinking about ageing. Might longer occupational lives be something to celebrate? As long as there may be a healthy work – life balance as a way of seizing the positive opportunities they present that could then contribute to making sustainable solutions possible.

For governments, the challenge is to change attitudes and preconceptions about what an ageing society means and to stimulate positive and innovative ideas and technologies to transform older lives. An opportunity may exist to seize the opportunity to rethink policies and approaches to public services as a way to foster true independence and choice for ageing adults and help them affirm and improve their own quality of life. For that to happen, society may need to explode the myth that midlife and ageing is a barrier to a positive contribution to the economy and citizenship through occupational engagement and a more active involvement in the community, both economically and politically.

Whilst Britain's equality legislation is meant to protect and promote fairness for all, the law may still fall short of doing so as far as age is concerned. When the single equality body was set up in 2004 it embedded fully in all policies directed towards ageing adults the values of active independence, quality, choice, occupation and work that were being championed in other areas. In the first quarter of the 21st century we may still question at times its effectiveness in this field.

Pause point

From your experience and understanding, do you question the effectiveness of the education system towards inequality and appreciation of old age?

Do you believe that ageing adults are treated with fairness and equality in modern day society? If not, list areas where inequality may still exist. If you agree with the statement, what themes may have contributed to improved equality for ageing adults?

May you personally and professionally play a part in ensuring such fairness and equality? If so, how?

Record your thoughts and reflect on current policies and legislative influences on this matter.

Life stage and the midlife transition

In order to further one's understanding, it is important to reflect on such views in the context of life stages and in particular, the midlife period (45–55 years old and beyond). However, it is proposed that a midlife stage should not be definitively determined, as each individual person may wish to define it for themselves. With this in mind and in the spirit of positive ageing and transitional retirement, some individuals within this age range may decide to prepare as many do, for an earlier than expected exit from organisational work or full-time employment. It needs to be acknowledged, however, that some authors question the existence of the midlife transition, and suggest it is a reflection of the personal construction and presentation of the life narrative and some may want to propose that no specific transition path can be laid out. However, the description and theorising of a midlife transition appears to be based on empirical evidence, albeit limited. In the context of this book, it is argued that the midlife transition is viewed as a plausible period in adult 'older' life.

It is important to look at what society appears to 'know' but not acknowledge about ageing, and to understand more about what is often referred to as the midlife transition as a way to consider some characteristics of this period. The work of the midlife transition is the personal facing, confrontation and accommodation of some or all of the experiences described above. These experiences constitute potential physical, psychological, emotional, and spiritual turning points, gaining new insights into one's self, a significant other or important life situations; this insight may become a motive that leads to positively redirecting, changing or improving one's life in recreation, leisure and in work. The turning point can take place against a background of a changed sense of reality, of time ahead and personal mortality. These experiences may constitute a growing exploration and sense of who one really is as a person, what one really wants out of life, as well as what the realities of the world and life are really like. The midlife and transition into retirement, therefore, may be seen as the process of reconciliation of gaps in the life structure, and the positive and dynamic actions that are needed to close them.

As retirees are no longer in full-time employment, may this change mean more time is spent engaging in alternative meaningful occupations and do people feel retirement has had a positive or negative effect on their health and well-being? Initially, ageing adults may enter into what was referred to earlier as the 'honeymoon' period, a time that may be characterised by enjoyment of free time, and the time needed for an individual to establish a stable retirement routine, whatever meaning that may have for the individual.

A number of general adult development studies have considered the midlife transition and the role of creativity, occupation and work. One of the earliest studies concerning midlife (Jaques 1965) examined it from the standpoint of the impact on creativity and work life of artists, although Jaques defined the midlife period as between 35 and 45 years old. The work of Levinson (1996) also comments on the potential impact of the midlife on creativity and work. Of interest however, this loosely defined period is often referred to as 'transition' by some, a 'crisis' by others. It is only fair to recognise that whilst the principle theorists use the word 'transition' they also acknowledge that a crisis can occur within a transition. This is particularly important when considering individual and collective crises in relation to uncertainties about the future beyond paid work.

In order to fully consider the balance between transition and crisis in this period, it may be useful to understand the characteristics of the midlife transition and the impact upon creativity and occupational engagement, since this period is described as containing a range of possible experiences that are physical, psychological and social in origin. No single event or occurrence is recognised as the starting point of the transition, and they may be experienced in any order. While these characteristics represent the way the experience of the midlife transition is reported, they are being written as reflecting the 'multiple meanings of age', the ways in which it will be encountered and experienced and in particular, when considering one's role in work and beyond.

When considering any transitional periods in one's life and the impact on creativity and occupations, many different authors have written about the way in which this period challenges individuals to recreate their identities in ways that may improve their sense of unity and purpose in life. This may involve individuals working through unresolved challenges and opportunities of earlier life, or revisiting and even affirming beliefs and goals for the future. The re-evaluation and assessment of one's situation may create a confrontation with aspects of the life structure not serving the desired direction and the opportunities that may exist to change. These can be part of the life structure, such as roles, relationships, or attitudes and values that have been developed or taken on in adult life. This said, some common themes may emerge from experiences of the midlife period as individuals may choose to enter a transitional period into 'occupation of choice' – namely retirement, or full or part ending of paid employment. These may include the following:

- A recognition of personal needs, dreams, hopes and ambitions in contrast to those which have hitherto been imposed in some way, often involving creative roles with a new generation of family members.
- Creativity of doing and also, more consciously, being in more aspects of our personal lives.
- Fulfil lost opportunities and achievements with a new sense of freedom and time.

- A new sense of the limitation of time and work or the choice of actions the individual seeks to accomplish in the time remaining to him/her.
- A lack of clarity of the actions and behaviours to which to devote ourselves, and attempts to reshape or redirect one's life accordingly.
- Re-directing a creative career in paid employment into a more creative occupation of choice, with no limits and much more freedom of time and choice.
- The capacity for being more creative shows itself for the first time.
- There may be a decisive change in both the quality and content of one's Creativeness.

However, whereas some move through this period with ease and without marked negative symptoms, for others the challenges may outweigh the opportunities.

What is important to remember, this need not be a painful period if one can learn how to harness one's creative ability and occupational growth. Some may possibly witness an increase in self-determination, ambition in occupational development, environmental mastery, choice over purpose in life and a continued desire for growth and creativity. There is little doubt that the literature on work and creativity produced in the past appears to have generated a potentially stereotypical message that creativity and the will to be occupationally engaged, declines with age. Even if there appears to be a stereotype, the evidence that creative ambition and achievement becomes more infrequent with advancing age is a premise that in most cases has been positively challenged.

Pause point – case study

Samira enjoyed a long career in corporate management and retired at the age of 60. Following retirement, she enrolled in a local college where she studied holistic therapies. Samira was initially intimidated by studying with people who were 40 years younger than herself, but she proved to be a model student, being voted Student of the Year on graduation. Samira now runs a successful company providing a range of holistic therapies in her local area.

> What factors may have influenced Samira to enrol on a college course?

> How do you think Samira felt in this educational environment after her career as a successful business woman?

> What challenges may Samira have had to work with in order to succeed?

> What qualities do you think Samira offered that resulted in her becoming student of the Year?

> Reflect on the above and start thinking whether there might have been added value had a retirement coach been in place to support Samira?

The importance of engaging in meaningful occupations has been explored widely by occupational scientists such as Wilcock (1998) who justifies that occupation is intrinsic to an individual's well-being. With this wisdom in mind, the next chapter will show that improvements in retirement transition can be more easily attained by building on perceptions of success, rather than focussing on failure. Important principles that guide appreciative inquiry practitioners in how to enhance a more positive approach are introduced with a particular focus on the application of the constructivist principle which will be explained.

CHAPTER 2

APPRECIATING TRANSITIONS

"I know you have plans, but reality is more exciting."
Andrew Machon

In this chapter, it is suggested that positive aspects of relationships and ourselves should be a starting point from which one can find a way forward. Based on these principles, appreciative inquiry, a model of 'intervention' and research that encourages affirmative action and behaviour will be introduced and explained.

Practical issues will be identified and discussed, for example ethics, individual and group factors. This chapter will introduce and give suggestions on how appreciative inquiry can be introduced as a way to enhance personal and professional development as a way to positively influence behaviours and personal approaches to ageing adults and retirement. Appreciative inquiry's potential is explored further and in more depth in Chapters 6 and 7.

Pause point

Ask yourself:

What do ageing adults uniquely offer?

What are your appreciative qualities, professionally and personally?

What are the qualities that may help individuals appreciate ageing?

Record what you may already know about appreciative inquiry and make a list of your own learning needs in order to better understand this particular approach.

Appreciative inquiry model of practice – The 4 D Model

In its original form, appreciative inquiry practitioners may have considered posing questions to the ageing adult or group participants, which would have focussed on occupational success (Cooperrider and Whitney 2005). Using this perspective, individuals are encouraged to build on one's own positive perceptions and experiences from the past or in the present, as a means to explore the potential for development and improvement (Fitzgerald, Murrell and Newman 2001). Such an approach may well contrast with other more traditional approaches which have primarily tended to focus on problem solving (Lewin 1951; Maguire 2001). The main challenge here is to remember that when the questioning or the dialoguing focuses excessively on problems, it can lead to poor self-esteem and defensiveness. Cooperrider and Whitney (2000) suggest that information emerging through adopting a problem- focussed interview or discussion can potentially be emotionally and psychologically damaging to the individual.

It is suggested that by focussing on life and occupational successes, the appreciative inquiry approach is more likely to empower the ageing adult to be more relaxed, excited and content with choices. One may feel accepted, more appreciated and valued and be seen to be sharing ownership of one's own occupational development. This is important as a way to acknowledge what may work for the best in their retirement, and in turn be able to articulate the necessary goals to achieve further affirmation and success (Boyd and Bright 2007), and move forward to agree an action plan to achieve identified goals (Fitzgerald et al. 2001). Professionals and retirement coaches aiming to help maximise on the required skills to achieve this, may collaborate with the ageing adult to work through the unconditional positive question allowing the retiree to focus on the most life-giving, life-sustaining aspects in this context, that of one's retirement experience (Ludema, Cooperrider and Barret 2001). The coaching interview and subsequent discussions may progress through four distinct stages enabling the process of enhancing success, affirming ideals and goals, and forward planning. These according to Ludema et al. (2001 p. 192) are:

- Discovery – where the focus is on identifying the most positive aspects of experience
- Dream – where ideal future development is envisioned based on this experience
- Design – where participants consolidate plans, and ways in which their ideal can be attained
- Destiny – plans are put into practice, and continue outside the group discussion

The appreciative inquiry approach may therefore motivate and empower ageing adults to change their perspective, enhance well-being and to improve health, outlook, situation, occupational balance and creativity.

(A practical application of the 4 D Model to a client is introduced later on in this chapter)

Appreciative inquiry and problem solving – the paradox

Since the appearance of appreciative inquiry, practitioners have attempted to describe it in numerous ways. It has been referred to as:

- a philosophy,
- a revolutionising force,
- a transformational change process,
- a life-giving theory and practice,
- a new world view.

Advocates of appreciative inquiry initiatives have called it 'hopeful and radical' in how complex humans and whole organisations can achieve sustainable and transformative change. Appreciative inquiry seems to satisfy the hunger so many people appear to have to create meaningful personal work and retirement lives that are both life affirming and inspirational.

Historically, appreciative inquiry's roots emerged from the work of David Cooperider in organisational development. He found problem solving to be an overused method for effecting change. As a result, he searched for ways to shift the prevailing strategy away from fixing problems that might or might not make an organisation better toward discovering what individuals or businesses wanted their organisation to be. Instead of focussing on what was not working, Cooperider began exploring what gave life to people and their workplaces when they were at their very best. He dared to ask questions about hope and inspiration and began to see that organisations were not problems to be solved but miracles and mysteries to be appreciated. The very same it is argued could be said about ageing adults in transitional retirement.

Cooperider believed in the importance of positive emotions in human development and emotional health, all supporting the power of positive imagery. He came to the conclusion that human systems show a remarkable tendency to move toward positive images of transitions into the future than those systems themselves created.

Cooperider and Strivastva (1987) saw appreciative inquiry as an approach to organisational analysis and learning that is intended for discovering, understanding, and fostering innovation. Ageing adults entering transitional retirement and those professionals supporting them through it, may find that it is 'life affirming' and that four propositions underlie its practice:

- Inquiry should begin with appreciation
- Inquiry into what is possible should yield information that can be used, applied, and validated in action
- Knowledge that appreciates 'what is' becomes proactive and can stir individuals to action

- Inquiry into human potential should be collaborative, assuming an immutable relationship between the process of inquiry and its content.

In essence, appreciative inquiry is a form of study that selectively seeks to locate, illuminate and highlight what are referred to as the 'life giving' forces of an organisation or an individual's existence; its positive core. Inherent in appreciative inquiry are assumptions about life, people, and the process of change itself.

These same assumptions (with minor adaptations), form the basis of the model of appreciative inquiry's (Cooperrider and Whitney 2005) belief that:

- In every society, organisation, group, community or individual something works;
- What people focus on becomes their reality;
- Reality is created in the moment, and there are multiple realities;
- The act of asking questions of a group, organisation or individual influences the group or individual in some way;
- People are more confident and comfortable in their journey to the future (the unknown) when they carry forward parts of the past (the known);
- If people carry parts of the past forward, those parts should be what is best about the past;
- It is important to value differences;
- The language people use creates their reality.

Appreciative inquiry in contrast to a problem solving approach can offer a much more holistic framework. It may hold the same core set of assumptions or beliefs; in essence, that human systems (and therefore ageing adults) will move toward the 'generative and creative images that reside in their most positive core – their values, visions, achievements and best practices. This potentially can link very closely to the principles that inform the basis of positive psychology.

Positive Psychology

The field of psychology has progressed its focus from the study of pathology to that of conditions and processes that contribute to affirmation, flourishing and optimal functioning. In the 90s, Martin Seligman from the American Psychological Association recognised psychology's focus on sickness and disease, with minimal attention being paid to what created energy, motivation and joy for people. But can one beckon the question that ageing adults can be happy about the past, content in the present, and hopeful about the future, though not necessarily all at the same time? An ageing adult's happiness can become pervasive if he/she reframes the narrative about a negative and unhappy past, a dissatisfying present, or a hopeless future. Seligman (2002) thought that if individuals make more conscious use of what he calls 'signature strengths' – those unique skills and abilities that individuals express easily – they can be happier in an authentic way. Seligman remained loyal to the notion that all emotions about the past are generated by thought and interpretation, and that humans can re-imagine or rethink past unhappy experiences in such a way that they become genuinely happier about them. To be content in one's well-being in an authentic way, Seligman believed that people must use their individual and unique strengths both to enhance and enrich their own personal and professional experience.

Seligman and Csikszentmihalyi (2000), advocated that the most optimum and enduring conditions that enable happiness, in particular amongst ageing adults, are:

- Friends
- Faith
- Family

This happiness is more ephemeral and has three main components:

- Pleasure – such as enjoying food
- Engagement – such as having an occupational focus
- Meaning – using one's strengths and discipline to make the world better in some way

Seligman and Csikszentmihalyi (2000) had, in a sense, anticipated the work in positive psychology relating to the experience of flow, the loss of self-preoccupation and the evaporation of time that occurs when an individual is deeply involved with some passionate occupation/activity. Positive psychology can inform the workings of the human spirit, mind, emotions and energy. To compliment this, appreciative inquiry can ground its pursuit in such disciplines. However it is important to remember that it does not deny the existence of unpleasant or negative aspects of life, nor does it want to see them through rose-coloured glasses. An appreciative inquiry approach to ageing adults believes in the positive approaches to learning and affirmative change. It offers the ageing adult and those professionals supporting them through transitional retirement a different way to explore their own deepest longings for happiness, health and well-being, time with their families and friends, and their most passionate occupational pursuits.

The relationship between appreciative inquiry and positive psychology

Appreciative inquiry terminology appears to relate closely to that of positive psychology, an established approach often used in some counselling and life coaching. Like appreciative inquiry, positive psychology believes in focussing on people's strengths as a major differentiator for organisations, practice and learning. Machon (2010) saw positive psychology as a discipline which centres on the study of positive emotion, positive character traits, and positive institutions thus adding a similar thread to one's understanding. In modern day, many would argue that society in general has already made a shift in focus from the study of the pathology of old age to the study of conditions and processes that contribute to optimum function (appreciative) with retirees. Whilst there appears, in general, to be a more positive enthusiasm about retirement, all too often the negative media bias tends to focus one's attention on the growing crisis with dementia care, loneliness and the negative economic burden of individuals taking early retirement.

It is only with the fairly recent heightened profile in the media of ageing adults continuing to engage fully in employment, leisure and recreational occupations, that this mindset has started to change for the positive. Using the principles of positive psychology and the appreciative movement, professionals and retirement coaches and society in general have been able to move towards a more positive attitude and approach when applied to coaching ageing adults during transitional retirement. Embracing this involves the retirement coach helping individuals to move away from a problem-solving focus (what is not being achieved effectively) towards working with issues with the added dimension of affirmation through the appreciative eye (what is being achieved effectively and described in detail in Chapters 6 and 7). It is important to remember that one's range of choice is ordinarily limited only by one's vision (Roberts and Machon 2015). The danger in seeing only problems is the potential preoccupation with the need to problem solve, finding the answer, which can limit the chance for the ageing adult to expand their vision further (Machon 2010). In truth, some problems cannot be solved and all that can be done is to facilitate the ageing adult to exist alongside the identified problem. In resisting the temptation to solve the problem with urgency, retirement coaches may empower the ageing adult to engage more fully in the transitional process with personal choice. However, a potential danger in this vision of change is that in thinking that one knows the correct answer, one may do so at the cost of reducing the potential skills of the ageing adult who has then to live with the result (Roberts and Machon 2015). This is not to deny the very practical need and role of the professional working as a retirement coach to explore problem solving as and when needed by the ageing adult, but to be aware of how the sole focus on problem solving can be profoundly limiting.

The foundation of appreciative learning and practice – the constructionist and the positive principles

The core assumptions of appreciative inquiry are deeply embedded and grounded in three main theoretical and research foundations – social constructionism, the new sciences, and research on the power of image and positive emotions.

There is the potential integration of five clearly defined principles that help guide appreciative inquiry practitioners in their focus on a positive approach (and the move away from a purely problem-solving path). These principles shape the philosophy that underlies appreciative inquiry:

1. constructionist principle
2. positive principle
3. simultaneity principle
4. poetic principle
5. anticipatory principle

The constructionist principles in action

In the context of transitional retirement, professionals and retirement coaches may aspire to enabling and empowering ageing adults to overcome challenges and even to assist in fixing or solving a particular problem or challenging situation.

Pause point and Terry's dilemma

For some years Terry has had a passion for golf and has been struggling with his ability to play the sport to the grade he would like to. In general, he describes himself as "just a bad player" compared to the other club members and he feels that he has not contributed anything to the team. A part of him wants to quit because he is disappointed and scared, golf is hard, and he does not know if he can do it anymore. Another part of him wants to try. It is one of those life lessons that is daunting to an ageing adult struggling with his transition and the belief he has in himself and his abilities, and daunting to his wife and grown up children, who want to see him realise his potential now he has the time to invest in his passion.

What do you think may be going on for Terry?

May his family have a role to better support him? If so, in what way?

How may you guide Terry to see his passion with more enthusiasm and acceptance of his level?

Make note of the dilemma faced by Terry, considering that it cannot be 'solved' because contained within it is the evolving mystery of life's potentiality. Who can predict the right outcome? On the one hand, quitting may lead Terry to a deepening sense of negativity about himself, or it may be a catalyst for him to try harder at something else.

Consider this statement and make some notes.

Consider if Terry does not quit, he might learn that he can achieve his goals despite initial setbacks and disappointments, but how?

Reality is created by one's choices in the moment or reactions to it, and people are usually presented with multiple paths.

What about the language Terry uses to describe himself? Did that really represent reality as others saw him? Did he have a balanced picture of himself?

In practice, one could interact daily with ageing adults who face their own dilemmas and who also may create their own interpretation of those situations. How may one best guide individuals in moving forward without limiting their options or taking away the opportunity for self–discovery? Some of the principles may be reassuring touchstones with which to guide and enable the support required by ageing adults in transitional retirement.

The ageing adult and the constructionist principle

As implied in its name, the constructionist theory is an expression of the social constructionist understanding of how ageing adults view the world. It indicates that theorists and practitioners are moving from a fixed, seemingly objective idea of the capacities of human potential to a more open exploration of possibilities. How ageing adults communicate, interact, create symbols, and construct metaphors with one another creates their reality. While ageing adults are able to define the physical world in objective terms, the social and psychological worlds are subjective; that is, they create meaning and reality through human communication and language.

The social constructionist view is equally liberating. When an ageing adult and indeed a retirement coach understands that their language and metaphors actually create their reality, they can use this as a catalyst for personal and professional change and growth. If the individual truly does not fully believe that life is predestined, one can mould and change it with thoughts and imagination. This may not be an easy concept for some ageing adults to embrace.

Three of the assumptions underlying appreciative inquiry are fundamental to this principle:

- What people focus on becomes their reality.
- The language people use creates their reality.
- In every individual, something works.

Knowing one's strengths, abilities, dreams and desires may be at the centre of every attempt ageing adults make at change. Knowing what is best about themselves may give people the foundations to be able to change in a positive, life enhancing way.

Recognising the constructionist principle

As a coach working with an appreciative aspect, much can be achieved to guide ageing adults toward a better knoledge of themselves by:

- Inquiring into their talents, past and present successes and un-met desires
- Listening to words, phrases, or metaphors that will guide them toward the reality they seek
- Helping them create a more holistic and balanced view of themselves
- Gently moving them from problem language to discovery and appreciative language
- Helping ageing adults create a clear image of the key attributes that they want to keep and build on for the future
- Encouraging ageing adults to take personal responsibility for what they know and how they know it

As an ageing adult's self–awareness and destiny are interwoven, an important aspect of appreciative learning and practice is the examination of who the ageing adult is now and how he/she talks about themselves in the past and present. It is all about what the ageing adult pays attention to and is curious about. This then forms the foundation for how they take action in creating their own future in retirement.

Appreciative language

Appreciative learning and practice can maximise on appreciative questions to help ageing adults to think about their past and current successes and what they would like to enhance in transitional retirement.

Here are some examples:

- Describe your three greatest accomplishments to date.
- What made these accomplishments stand out for you?
- What have you incorporated into your current actions from your past accomplishments?
- How can you use what you've learned from these accomplishments to assist you in making future changes?
- List five adjectives that describe you at your best.
- What situations tend to bring out your best?
- What are you learning and accepting about yourself at present?

Such questions can be key in helping ageing adults free themselves from outmoded habits and old beliefs. As they begin to understand how their language and actions have focussed their reality in specific ways, they may shift to new words and metaphors to describe where they are and where they want to go. When applying coaching skills, health and social care professionals may have the potential to become catalysts to enable this type of change through exploring and employing the language that supports the constructionist belief that ageing adults can create and change their life through their thinking and imagining.

Recognising the positive principle

There are four significant ways in which the retirement coach may apply an affirmative, positive principle and belief in the potential of ageing adults to enable them to be at their best:

- Through affirmation and appreciation.
- Nurturing their expression of positive emotions.
- Helping them enhance their reflected best self-portrait.
- Building virtuous cycles (positive self-reinforcing cycles in how they view their own thoughts, emotions and actions) – this is the opposite of 'vicious cycles' in which a bad thing leads to a worse one.

Appreciative practice is designed to create powerful social experiences that can help ageing adults discover the best about themselves. The expression of the constructionists' principle is fundamental to ensuring that ageing adults move toward an appreciative perspective of themselves and their situation, that they move toward appreciative language in speaking about themselves and that they build a more holistic and balanced view of themselves. The positive principle involves helping ageing adults generate and express positive emotions; urging them to create a sustainable positive connection to others; providing appreciative and challenging jolts for them in the form of insights, experimentation, and new practices; and helping those in transitional retirement build a sense of one's own potency and potential as creators of their own future.

Case study applying the 4 D Model

Paul is a 68-year-old retired mechanic whose passion has been his motorbikes. He has been in intensive rehabilitation following a motorbike accident three months ago in which he suffered injury to his left upper and lower limbs. His left index finger and thumb have been amputated, and the accident has left him with mobility problems.

Paul, having been discharged, is looking for a retirement coach to help him adjust to independent living, and make the transition into retirement effectively. He is also wanting support and guidance in relation to his anxiety around his financial situation and future income potential.

In your initial meeting with Paul he starts off by saying:

"It started for me when I realised that following my motorbike accident and despite all of my best efforts, I was not making any progress to come to terms with leaving my garage and my old job. My frustrations and concerns grew to the point that I was beyond worrying about the potential embarrassment of admitting my struggles to friends, colleagues, and therapists. I'm also petrified of not being financially independent."

Paul tells you that he is feeling demoralised because he has been unable to carry on with his recreational and leisure occupation of renovating old motorbikes, the work he once loved. His situation has become so critical that he will soon be faced with decisions he does not want to make. He says that he has worked very hard and given away a great deal to local community groups in an effort to make his work known, but the financial benefit is not coming back to him as he had hoped, thus making him feel very depressed. He anticipates that his injuries will not challenge his ability to follow his passion and his occupation of choice. Paul hands his garage over to his son, but he still has some input into its management.

Potential assumptions thus far

Assumptions at this stage are based on Paul's remarks. His main concern is his ability to return to his passion of renovating motorbikes and securing his future financial situation.

Applying the principles of the 4 D Model of appreciative inquiry to Paul

1) Discovery (what is)

Example of affirmative interview questions:

- Tell me, what are the most positive things that have happened to you following your accident?
- Have you had any pleasant surprises in the way people react to you?
- Describe your three greatest accomplishments to date and how can you use what you've learned from these accomplishments to assist you in making future changes?
- What made them stand out for you?
- What are the five most positive things in your life?
- Who are the key supportive people in your life and what do they provide for you?
- List five adjectives that describe you at your best.
- What energises you?
- What would you like to contribute to the world?
- What are you most wanting to achieve in the next three years?

As you can see, there are no questions about problems or concerns or issues or anything that was negative.

Following these questions, the insights for Paul may include:

- I survived and lived through a major trauma.
- I have a zest for life.
- I'm a survivor in life.
- I can find humour/hope irrespective of my accident.
- I am loved and cared for by family and friends.
- I'm getting practical advice and support to adapt.
- I love my hobby and want to get back to it as I can see my input into people's lives makes a difference.
- I tend to do a lot of giving to others but not much asking for myself.
- I have skills and experience and I am employable.

Paul says:

"… my coach continues to ask me positive, very probing, very challenging questions around all my issues, all the while helping me feel more positive about taking new actions that could achieve more successful outcomes for each issue. Every question, and every agreed action is geared toward trying something that fits with my strengths, values, and vision and that would lead to a positive and appreciative outcome."

Applying the principles of a problem-solving approach – identify the main challenges/problems.

Building on the above, and in partnership with Paul, the coaching interview will identify the main challenges and problem areas in all aspects of his personal, occupational, social and spiritual life.

For example:

- Mobility
- Activities of daily living
- Cognitive /concentration
- Memory
- Personal and professional relationships
- Recreation – return to hobby
- Range of movement
- Dexterity/nerve damage
- Mental state
- Emotional state

2) Dream (what might be)

Paul begins to shift his focus from immediate awareness of how he was changing in his life and recreational life to how he wants to change his life and occupations. Once the discoveries are well underway, the coach may start moving Paul towards a dream or vision for his life, hobbies and retirement.

Paul states:

"I handed over my garage to my son when I retired but I still do some of the ordering, audits and paperwork for him. I realise that if I continue to behave in the way I've been with respect to my issues and processes at home and my motorbikes, my vision won't be achieved, I won't get fit again and my private and retirement life will be compromised."

The retirement coach may ask Paul to write a list of what he needs, and what vision he wants with his occupation of choice and retirement. What are his dreams?

Paul, in dialogue with his wife, came to realise that the financial reward for his business involvement with his son is not what he dreamed about, but felt uneasy about how to bring this up. Paul decided that it would be ideal for him to engage his son in his own dream for the business.

3) Design (what should be)

In preparation for intervention, Paul and the coach craft a strategy using his strengths and expertise to build a personal and retirement life. Paul takes coaching very seriously and has developed a marketing strategy to further his vision around what he is good at. As a result of experimenting and thinking of a way forward, Paul reports that given his current physical and mental state he has decided to take some specific action steps:

- Phasing a handover of his business
- Create a positive call for action (what support he requires to fulfil his dream with his motorbikes)

Action plan and intervention

Based on and building on the stages thus far – Paul and the coach explore and design an action plan to include the specific occupation-based tools and other resources to help Paul fulfil his vision and future needs.

Outcome of process:

- Links with significant others in his life
- Activities of daily living
- Address mobility and fitness issues – dexterity/range of movement (variety of activities)
- Economic needs
- Cognitive/concentration/memory
- Recreational needs
- Physical needs
- Psychological needs
- Spiritual needs
- Emotional needs
- Environmental needs
- Personal/sexual life
- Professional needs
- Consider other agencies to involve

4) Destiny – (what will be)

Once Paul can clearly envision his dream for his life and retirement, he may need to go about designing and building that dream and affirm what will be.

Here are Paul's tangible outcomes and benefits realised as a result of the coaching relationship.

Paul states:

"At the beginning of my coaching, I had all to lose; my physical and mental health, plus my personal and recreational retirement aspirations in particular with my wife and son. At the beginning I felt all was lost, now I'm physically on the mend, getting independent in both body and mind."

He adds:

"I credit my coach and her positive questioning, and her belief in enabling to understand more about myself and how to utilise my own natural strengths to create more and better possibilities for myself and my hobby. I now have a real capacity for creating a mutually beneficial existence for me and my occupation of choice in my life. I have a much more positive, appreciative awareness and much higher energy around my strengths, and I know how to use them. My vision is now firmly within my grasp, and tangible results have already occurred."

Possible solutions – adapting and evaluating

Progressing with dynamic and affirmative coaching, Paul continues to work on his needs and vision. As Paul successfully progresses and heals, the process has to incorporate the aspects of Paul's original problems/challenges that cannot be solved. However, he can now adapt to living with these unresolved themes in his life.

The process continues until Paul is referred on to other agencies with the vision of eventual independence.

Pause point

Reflect on the 4 D model and offer a critique of its application with Paul.

Would you add or do anything differently?

With a better understanding of the 4 D Model – highlight its potential and also its challenges when applied.

Having explored appreciative transitions and the potential use of one model of practice, the following chapter aims to highlight the key issues raised within the literature on ageing adults' activity and occupations. The literature review analyses the nature of the modern day ageing population and introduces and discusses a number of theories of ageing. Active ageing strategies will also be introduced with reference to some national, international and local initiatives.

CHAPTER 3

MEANINGFUL, CREATIVE ACTIVITY AND OCCUPATION OF CHOICE

"I am an acorn who dreams of the oak."
Machon (2005)

This chapter aims to highlight the key issues raised within the literature on issues of creativity, activity and occupation in later life whilst considering aspects of spirituality and its potential importance in this context. A description of an increasing ageing population is discussed with reference to a number of acknowledged theories of ageing, such as structured dependency, disengagement theory, activity theory and continuity theory, as a way to better understand meaning.

Ageing and creativity

From an occupational scientist's perspective, when considering creativity and one's understanding of occupation, the engagement in meaningful and purposeful activity is seen in the wider context of everything that we do – both paid and unpaid. It is concerned with understanding humans as occupational beings and the relationship between occupation and health (Yerxa, Clark, Jackson, Parham, Pierce, and Stein 1998). Key theorists such as Csikszentmihalyi (1996) supported questioning the perception of a decline in creative and occupational activity over time and reported that productivity did not decline with age and that, if anything, it actually increased. The perception of Csikszentmihalyi's research participants were primarily seen as being in the midlife transition, that their ability to work was largely unimpaired as they aged and that their goals remained as significant as they had been in earlier life. Of interest, concerns about health or well-being were largely absent from his interviews with participants. Their attitudes to physical health were largely positive and their ability associated with crystallised intelligence were perceived as increasing, for example "…making sensible judgements, recognising similarities across different categories, using induction and logical reasoning" (p. 213). A significant positive development in personal traits when engaging in occupation was reported as "diminishing anxiety, over performance, being less driven, exhibiting more courage, confidence and risk taking" (p. 215). In the study, it is noted that women reported twice as many positive outcomes than men. Comments from these participants concerning their relationship to domains of performance were uniformly positive. "It seems the promise of more and different knowledge never lets us down; symbolic domains remain always accessible and their rewards remain fresh until the end of life" (p. 218). Csikszentmihalyi, however, acknowledged a contradiction, in that his research participants were actively and deeply engaged in meaningful occupation they found continuingly exciting. Yet the fulfilment of the occupation many were engaged in would be unattainable to them in the future. He suggested "these people never run out of exciting goals" (p. 220), "… there was "very little dwelling on the past success, everyone's energies were focussed on tasks still to be accomplished" (p. 221).

Two decades ago, Lindauer, Orwoll and Kelley (1997) made an important contribution to articulating what else may be happening to the experience and performance of creativity and work in midlife and beyond. In a questionnaire survey they asked 88 prominent graphic artists in the 40–70 age range to review performance and characteristics of their work over a period of time. There were consistent reports of positive changes to the quality, quantity and content of creative work with only marginal declines beyond the age of 60. The primary reasons described included the following (p. 134–136):

- increased skill and improved techniques that came from continuing professional development
- the concept of lifelong learning and the discovery of new working materials
- increase in time available to them due to a decline in family responsibilities

- an increased "acceptance of themselves, their occupations and their abilities" – and an acceptance of others
- A "reduced concern with other people's criticisms or evaluations" was also reported as a source of work
- "the freedom to attempt work they may previously have been deterred from trying" (p. 139)

This presents an important contrasting perspective to the recognised peak of social acclaim that occurs commonly in the first half of the 40s and the midlife transition. This research of 20 years ago by Lindauer et al. (1997) is still of relevance as it suggests that social acclaim is less of a priority creatively than before – and that other priorities emerge over time.

For individuals, it is argued that longer life is a blessing when the extra years are productive, fulfilling and active, especially in transitional retirement. They do not have to be years of inaction and exclusion. It is argued that a personal responsibility rests on individuals to plan and provide for a different life-course that is also better. For business, a changing customer base offers new markets and opportunities.

In some services that are crucial to retaining independence, ageing adults are still often treated as passive recipients rather than active consumers with their own views about their needs. Chronological age does not necessarily have to be a bar to choice and control of one's own personal life to the maximum possible level, particularly in relation to creativity and involvement in activities and occupations of choice. Whatever the results of published studies and the characteristics currently proposed for occupation and creativity, it needs to be acknowledged that the midlife in the context of leading into older age remains a relatively new area of research interest, with comparatively few research studies on which to base the claims of a universal midlife transition. As people live longer, one could argue, therefore, that the midlife transition may occur later on in chronological age, for example, as transitional retirement occurs. Theoretical sources may argue that a focus in this time period on productive output and social acclaim is inadequate to portray and understand the events occurring within occupations, work and the creative process. This time period in the ageing adult's life is under explored theoretically compared with childhood and adolescence. Those sources suggest that attention to the characteristics of activity and creativity in this time period, and that the phenomenology of creative work indicative of the experience of ageing would yield new understandings of creativity.

It appears that ageing adults are increasingly becoming key players in occupational success and, as such, society has a huge role to play in enabling communities and individuals to adjust effectively to a new balance of life, especially as an ageing demographic is resulting in a larger proportion of ageing adults living in modern day communities. With that in mind, ageism should be discarded. To dispel ageism, individuals in the midlife and beyond may be seen as being of value to society, but what is this value? Ageing adults live through what is often termed the midlife crisis. This, in truth, may be perceived as a crisis for some in which most of today's workforce live, work and orientate themselves, for it is a crisis that may extend somewhere between the age of 35 and 55. The value of ageing adults is both in living this experience and with hindsight, being able to place it within a healing and creative context.

Pause point

Think about your own attitude to ageing in relation to success and creativity:

Have these changed over time? If so, why?

Can you identify a time when you became aware of your changing priorities in this midlife phase?

How did these changing attitudes present themselves in everyday life and the activities you engaged in?

Write a personal reflection and record what factors may have influenced your attitude. Were there any significant situations that may have offered you insights?

Theories of ageing

In response to concerns about the implications of this ageing demographic, the field of gerontology, the study of ageing, emerged in the middle of the last century. This field of study has greatly expanded since that time. Initial theories considered the problems of ageing to be issues of personal adjustment, such as:

- Disengagement Theory,
- Activity Theory and, then,
- Continuity Theory.

Later developments acknowledged the importance of structure on the ageing process, namely, the Structured Dependency and Political Economy theories.

Disengagement theory

Cumming and Henry (1961 cited in Gilleard and Higgs 2000) suggest that ageing adults withdraw from social and economic interactions as a chosen pathway or as a natural progression. The theory suggests that this withdrawal is a natural process of ageing as it enables younger, more efficient workers to enter the workforce and allows ageing individuals to be freed of demanding social responsibilities because "as the ageing process develops, individuals become increasingly self-absorbed … thus, disengagement is viewed as a natural and desirable outcome" (Estes, Biggs and Phillipson, 2003 p. 14). This does not, however, explain the experiences of those ageing adults who do not wish to disengage as they age. Ageing adults who do not want to disengage in old age are described as anomalies and labelled either "unsuccessful adjusters to old age, off-time disengagers, or members of a biological or psychological elite" (Phillipson & Baars 2007 p. 71).

Activity theory

This theory opposes the above stance taken by 'Disengagement Theory', as there also emerged a school of thought that accepted ageing adults wish to remain actively involved in society as the norm rather than irregular behaviour. This phenomenon was described by Havighurst (1963 cited in Reed, Stanley, and Clarke 2004 p. 19) as "older…happiest with their lives were those who had remained active and engaged with social life. This could involve maintaining existing activities and relationships or … developing new ones". The resulting Activity Theory is based on the belief that "psychological and social well-being could be enhanced by involvement in social roles and activities" (Estes et al. 2003 p. 13). More specifically, ageing adults would be more satisfied and could even live longer if they "keep up their level of activity appropriate to their middle years and if they replace abandoned activities with new ones" (Künemund & Kolland 2007 p. 173). Estes et al. (2003) acknowledge, "activity theory has gained widespread acceptance in professional circles and among ageing adults as an antidote to the problem of ageing identity" (p. 68). However, a study by Everard (1999) explored the relationship between activity and well-being in ageing adults and suggests that while there is a positive relationship between well-being and activity engagement, it is the "reasons for the activities themselves (that) seem more important than simply keeping busy with many activities" (p. 335). The findings do not support Activity Theory as the study found a negative influence on well-being with greater levels of activity and those that were used simply to 'pass the time'.

Continuity theory

This is a further theory that considers people's changing patterns of activity as they age. This "assumes that humans tend to maintain patterns of their former lifestyle, their sense of self-esteem, and their values even after retirement from paid work" (Atchley 1989 cited in Künemaund &

Kolland 2007 p.174). This theory explains how individuals' sense of identity can be maintained into old age by engaging in activities that have been meaningful throughout their lives. This may include the adoption of new activities but, while Activity Theory encourages this to compensate for activities that can no longer be performed, Continuity Theory stresses the importance of the meaningfulness of the new activity with relation to identity, and the process of adapting activities to retain this sense of self. Pushkar et al. (2010) further explored the relationship between activity and older age by performing a study over two years following participants' retirement. The study aimed to test Continuity and Activity Theories in relation to the positive and negative affect caused by activity engagement. While the influence of Activity Theory was suggested by the positive affect gained by enhanced engagement, this study found that "continuity and affect is dominant" (p. 47). In support of Everard (1999), Pushkar, Chaikelson, Conway, Etezadi, Giannopoulus, Li and Wrosch (2010 p. 48) indicate the importance of the meaning of chosen activities but also highlights the "harmful effects of decreasing activity", as suggested by the Disengagement Theory.

It is clear that Disengagement Theory, Activity Theory and Continuity Theory agree that changing individual activity patterns are natural and necessary in old age, although there is disagreement regarding the nature of this adjustment.

Pause point

Think about the three theories detailed above:

Can you identify any of these in the behaviours of ageing adults that you know or are working with?

Which theory do you think most accurately describes these changes?

If you are an ageing adult yourself, can you identify any of these theories in your own lifestyle?

When critiquing all three theories, some could argue that there is an apparent lack of consideration given to the structural components of society, such as economic and political influence.

Reflect on this and offer your own personal critique of the three named theories.

This individualised approach by social gerontologists was described by Townsend (1981) as 'acquiescent functionalism' in which the individual nature of ageing is experienced within a societal structure, rather than being manufactured by it. One approach that considers the economic and political influences on ageing is Structured Dependency Theory. This is based on the foundation that "the dependency of older adults is being manufactured socially" (Tinker 1997 p.263). Townsend (1981) suggested that older adults' opportunities for engagement and participation in later life have been limited by institutionalised age discrimination through the implementation of policies, such as those that enforced mandatory retirement and, therefore, limited the possibility of enhancing income in old age.

Ageing adults and the state pension system

Although this book does not aim to focus on the economics of ageing, an understanding of the State Pension system in the United Kingdom as an example may be useful due to its influence on Structured Dependency theory. The pension system was introduced in the United Kingdom by the Old Age Pensions Act in 1908, and it afforded a means-tested benefit to people of 70 years of age from 1st January 1909. But the United Kingdom's pension structure as we know it today has its foundation in the National Insurance Act of 1946, that introduced a contributory pension for all citizens and set the ages at which this could be claimed at

60 for women and 65 for men. The seed for this change in policy was the Beveridge Report; written by Sir William Beveridge in 1942 and entitled 'Social Insurance and Allied Services'. In it he detailed plans to introduce a basic state pension (BSP) to ensure that all United Kingdom citizens were brought out of poverty in their old age.

During the years since 1948, the BSP has been reviewed and refined repeatedly, particularly in recent years. Until recently the situation in the United Kingdom remained that men reach pension age at 65 whereas, until 6th April 2010, women still reached pension age at 60 years. However, the Pensions Act 1995 reviewed the State Pension Age (SPA) of women describing that from 6th April 2010 the age for women will steadily rise until 2020 when it will equal that of the male members of the population,

65 years, although this will only apply to those women born after 5th April 1950. So, it is planned that from 6th April 2020, there will be equity between the pension ages of all men and women in the United Kingdom. This is not to remain in place indefinitely, however, as the British Government has detailed plans in the Pensions Act 2007 to increase the pension age further in the coming decades. Between 2024 and 2046 it is expected that the pension age will increase steadily every 10 years. This will result in the pension age of both men and women being 68 years by 2046. However, more recent forecasts suggest that this timescale has been condensed to meet the 68-year target by 2039. It is important to recognise that pension age is not the same as the age at which an individual may retire, as retirement can occur before or after pension age, dependent on each individual's personal situation (Bozio et al. 2010; Directgov 2010).

Ageing adults and the Structured Dependency theories

Gilleard and Higgs (2000) described such Structured Dependency theories expounded by Phillipson, Townsend and Walker in the United Kingdom, and the associated Political Economy Approach popularised by the work of Estes, Minkler, Myles and Olson in the United States, as agreeing that "the dependent social position of older adults is created by social policy… (and) as a consequence, it is discriminatory and disadvantageous state policies, not biology, that dominate the lives of older people" (p. 13).

As social structures and policy impact on ageing adults, it is acknowledged that there are some limitations to the explanatory power of Activity Theory, Disengagement Theory and Continuity Theory. It could be argued that both Disengagement Theory and Activity Theory stem from a structural (normative) belief that ageing adults are not productive members of society and while Disengagement Theory supports withdrawal from previous roles and responsibilities, Activity Theory encourages the opposite, that individuals should participate in a variety of activities for all long as possible. However, these theories, along with Continuity Theory "ignore the restrictions on the individual due to power structures and patterns of inequalities in society" (Bowling 2008 p. 293).

Similarly, Structured Dependency theory cannot fully explain the vast levels of heterogeneity within the ageing population without accepting that, although state structures will certainly impact either positively or negatively on the ageing population, individuals also have the opportunity to exert personal choice and free will throughout the ageing process. This is recognised by Estes et al. (2003) who accept that the "playing down of human agency" (p. 118) is a prevalent criticism of the structured dependency philosophy. Estes et al. (2003) also recognise that the field of Critical Gerontology, which emerged at the end of the twentieth century, now accepts that while structure has the greatest influence on the experience of ageing, personal perceptions must also be considered as an understanding of both aspects is "essential for social action and progressive change" (p. 3).

Pause point – case study

Denise is a 65-year-old teacher. She wanted to be a teacher from an early age but, due to family commitments, was unable to follow this career path until her 40s, eventually securing her first teaching position at the age of 45. Just 20 years later, Denise was forced to retire as her school would not allow her to continue employment after the age of 65.

Were the authorities within their right to force Denise to retire at 65? If not, what could Denise do about it?

How do you think Denise felt about this decision?

Which theory of ageing influenced this decision most directly?

What message were the school authorities sending Denise, and how do you think that may impact on her health and well-being?

What support would you offer someone in a similar situation? How would you enable Denise to positively move forward?

Research your government's current position on mandatory retirement and how this may change over time. Reflect on how this could impact your own situation.

While the above discussion examines some of the gerontological theories that explain changes in activity patterns in later life, Katz (2000) undertook a study of residents in a retirement resort in Canada to examine this phenomenon in practice. The results suggest that levels of engagement in activity in older age had become, in some environments, a means of defining an individual's worth, in a similar way that Structured Dependency theory suggests that people are labelled as productive or unproductive members of society, based on their economic contribution. Individual notions of 'activity' can be a source of conflict with some people participating in 'anti- activity activities', for example, passive activities such as watching television, or those that are seen as disreputable, such as gambling. The paper notes that failure to conform and participate in organised and accepted activities can result in individuals feeling pressured to do so against their wishes. Katz (2000) accepts that "most gerontological and policy discourses pose activity as the 'positive' against which the 'negative' forces of dependency, illness and loneliness are arrayed" (p. 147). However, when addressing these needs from a policy perspective, structural and individual aspects should be considered to enable those ageing adults who wish to remain active but are unable to do so, whether due to ill health, disability or restricted income, to achieve a satisfying level of engagement. As a response to this need, Active Ageing philosophy has been illustrated in a variety of global and local policies and strategies.

Active ageing

The concept of active ageing is not a recent development. Back in 2002, for example, WHO published its 'Active Ageing: A Policy Framework' document as part of the Second United Nations World Assembly on Ageing. It was designed to "inform discussion and the formulation of action plans that promote health and active ageing" (WHO 2002 p. 2). The document was established to provide guidance for world governments to adapt to the ageing population by embracing "a life course perspective that recognises the important influence of earlier life experiences on the way individuals age" (WHO 2002 p. 6). It was developed with due consideration given to the United Nations Principles for Older People, namely, independence, participation, care, self-fulfilment and dignity (United Nations [UN] 1992). WHO defines active ageing as "the process of optimising opportunities for health, participation and security in order to enhance quality of life as people age" (WHO 2002 p. 12), and suggests a number of ways in which this may be achieved, including promoting physical activity, lifelong learning and increased access to employment, with an overarching belief that "an active ageing approach seeks to eliminate age discrimination and recognise the diversity of older populations" (WHO 2002 p. 46).

Within the United Kingdom as an example, the influence of the 'Active Ageing: A Policy Framework' document (WHO 2002) was reflected in the development of policies and strategies of the Welsh Assembly Government, such as 'The Strategy for Older People in Wales' (WAG 2003), and 'The National Service Framework for Older People in Wales' (WAG 2006). These documents support the philosophy of active ageing in a number of ways, for example, by tackling age discrimination, promoting physical activity and challenging dependency. The links between structure and agency is demonstrated in all of these documents as, although they recommend strategies that are government or community led, they also acknowledge the heterogeneity of the ageing population and the necessity to adapt services to meet the changing needs of individuals.

Pause point

Compare developments in Wales to those in the rest of the United Kingdom. Research whether policies and initiatives in the four nations of the United Kingdom are similar or not to those in neighbouring European countries and some of the other countries of the world, such as Australia and the United States.

Record your findings and decide how differing policies and directives may influence the quality of life of its ageing population.

Although 'active ageing' is clearly a paradigm that long has been accepted by governments and international organisations, such as WHO and the UN, Bowling (2008) raises the concern that the concept of 'active ageing' is not clearly defined and understood by the general public, which is an important issue as one of its aims is to engage ageing adults and encourage active participation in economic, civic and social activities. To explore ageing adults' perceptions of 'active ageing', Bowling carried out a study in which a sample of ageing adults were questioned about their understanding of 'active ageing' and asked to rate their own levels of activity. The results suggest that the participants generally "perceived active ageing more in terms of actively maintaining their mental and physical health and wider well-being" (Bowling 2008 p. 299). Although differences were highlighted by the ageing adults who were more likely to indulge in what has previously been discussed as the passive activity of reading, it is suggested by Bowling that this is an adaptation to their inability to engage in more active pursuits due to increased frailty and declining health. Less impact on perceptions of active ageing were recorded by differences in socio-economic status, importance of finance, age, gender or marital status. As such, although differences between individuals may restrict the way in which they can participate, such as ageing adults reading more, their perceptions did not change significantly. This suggests that perceptions of active ageing are individualised and can fluctuate over the life course as people's abilities and priorities change.

Bowling (2008) also suggests that as the majority of participants focussed on participating in active activities, their understanding of active ageing "reflects the predominance of a functional model of society, and reflected ageist social norms, which exclude frailer people from participation" (p. 300). This exclusion of frailer people from participation is not supported in the documents discussed above, as WHO and the UN recognise the importance of including frailer people in active ageing strategies. This highlights the disparity between the aims of the 'active ageing' framework and the understanding of the 'active ageing' concept by the participants in this study.

Pause point

Think about the activities that you personally enjoy:

Are these considered good/active activities or bad/passive activities?

How would being judged by your activity choice make you feel?

Do you judge others based on the activities in which they engage?

Activities often have meaning, value and hopefully may signify a great deal spiritually to ageing adults. A spiritual journey is different for everyone, but each ageing adult, according to Bash (2004 p. 4), can "formulate his or her own spiritual co-ordinates, sometimes consciously and sometimes not … spirituality is therefore an elastic, subjective description about a person and about the way they express their humanity".

Spirituality and ageing adults

Spirituality may mean different things to different people and is probably recognised in most cultures as an essential component of a person – a centred and holistic interaction, which can have a significant impact on an ageing adult's health, well-being and occupation. Historically, the term spirituality has been used synonymously with religion, and may have both negative and positive feelings attached to it. Spirituality is described as an abstract concept in an abundance of literature published on the subject of spirituality and spiritual need. Within health and social care, it is argued that there is more recognition that spirituality greatly influences peoples' overall health and well-being, and the subject was included in the recommendations of the Francis report (2013) in the United Kingdom. In a modern and progressive society an ageing adults' cultural heritage will potentially influence his or her creativity and spiritual expression, especially during the change process of transitional retirement.

Affirmative human experiences and feelings such as love, hope, dreams, will and desires may not be easy to analyse and at times may be difficult to measure and to quantify. However, when applying an appreciative approach, professional practitioners as coaches may be best placed to assist ageing adults and to recognise and appreciate their spiritual needs.

In order to genuinely grasp the importance and meaning of the spiritual experiences and existence of ageing adults as individuals entering transitional retirement, appreciative inquiry as an approach can equip professionals and ageing adults themselves to better understand their experiences, their values and belief systems. Appreciative inquiry not only provides a framework to acquire new positively focussed skills but also, and perhaps more importantly, the development of a fresh way of viewing life, their spiritual beliefs such as their values, hopes, dreams and their level of connectedness to the process of transitional retirement. This is discussed further in Chapter 6, and in the context of a new and innovative 3 'Eye' Model of practice.

Spirituality and religion

For many ageing adults, religion and spirituality may not be interchangeable terms. They are often linked together for the sake of convenience and it is because of this that differentiation between the two has become notoriously difficult, thereby causing confusion. Professional practitioners and coaches should recognise that specific religions may have certain unique characteristics and rituals that play an essential role in the lives of some of the individuals with whom they are working.

Spirituality, however, is seen as individualistic, unique and less to do with doctrines, ideas or even rituals (Kliewer and Saultz 2006). It is more to do with inner feelings, emotions, the heart, connectedness with self, others and nature, and the well of inner strength from which a person draws support at a time of crisis (Slay 2007). In the context of transitional retirement, potential challenges may be seen as a crisis by some but as an opportunity by others. As such, a full spiritual and religious context is likely to be central to ageing adults' lives, particularly at times of change.

The mind-body-spirit paradigm

It is argued that the philosophical principles of professional practice are informed by engagement in aspects of person-centred practice and holism, including biological, psychological, social, emotional, environmental and spiritual factors. When providing support that seeks to address all such dimensions of an ageing person's life, these dimensions may have equal importance to an ageing person's occupational functioning and well-being. Age and life experience may be important in spiritual development as some ageing adults may begin to reflect inward to explore the more spiritual aspects of the self. Age may allow retirees to consider the reality of one's own mortality, for example, which in turn may open more opportunities to fulfil more creative occupational opportunities.

It is clear that no single gerontological theory of ageing can illustrate the diverse experiences that are demonstrated by members of the ageing population. While some of the historical studies cited agree that activity engagement can have a positive effect on well-being in later life, it is the meaning of the activity, rather than the quantity that appears to be the most influential factor. In the next chapter, the concept of occupational choice and activity engagement will be explored further by considering the impact of gender and marital status in later life.

MARITAL STATUS, GENDER, SEXUAL ORIENTATION, OCCUPATIONAL ENGAGEMENT AND RETIREMENT TRANSITION

"Aging sexually and adjusting to old age sexually are important topics for many people, but rarely do we get a chance to work them out. Contemporary culture tends to consider all topics, especially sexuality, in terms of externals and behaviours. What is right and proper behaviour?
Thomas Moore (2017)

This chapter explores the potential significance and impact of gender, culture, sexual orientation and marital status in terms of considering engagement in meaningful activities during the transitional life period of retirement. This chapter will look at adversity, resilience and transformational growth towards retirement and beyond. It is important to acknowledge here that there may be cultural elements and influences of importance, as precisely how to define 'retirement' in a cross-culturally valid way may be problematic. A seeming familiarity with how ageing adults make the transition into retirement may challenge our ability to recognise its specific features and the problem. Do ageing adults in all societies and cultures 'retire' as such? May the very notion of retirement have a universal focus? Is it possible that retirement may be a strange phenomenon to some non-Western cultures? Are gender, marital status and sexuality of importance in such discussions? In exploring these themes, this chapter plants some questions for the reader to explore and reflect on themselves, keeping in mind that culture, values, beliefs and perceptions are very personal and subjective human traits in a field that would value more actual research data.

Gender

Some studies have shown that gender plays a great part in the way individuals react to life changes, such as retirement (Bowling 2008; Barnes and Parry 2004), so in general may one expect women to react differently to men? Some literature demonstrates the influence that stereotypical gender roles in society have on peoples' career choices at a younger age. Although such defined societal norms may have changed over recent years, with more women in the workplace and a uniform retirement age being introduced in the UK, ageing adults may still have defined gender roles and expectations.

Pause point

Reflect on men and women you know who have retired.

> Do you think that gender has been an influencing factor in their transition? If so, why? And in what way?

> Do you think culture and education play a part in stereotyping? If so, how?

Record your thoughts and identify ways and areas where stereotypical gender and cultural norms have positively changed over time.

Some studies have also highlighted trends in activity choice between genders, such as differences in household tasks and leisure activities. For example, it can be argued that men prefer to engage in household maintenance activities but do not participate as much in creative activities, as previous studies in the United Kingdom and Denmark (Legarth, Ryan and Avlund 2005; Ball et al. 2007) support such patterns. Creativity, however, may not be limited to specific activities, and can encompass activities such as decorating a house or building a shed. The individual's perception of whether an activity is or is not creative is paramount. Occupational therapy theory, for example, shows that activity can be either self-care, productivity or leisure and it is the meaning given to the activity that is important. While one person may see decorating a room as a creative leisure pursuit, another may feel that it is an unwelcome chore. As such, the benefits of the activity would be very different to these individuals. There are clearly many men who engage in traditional creative activities as this is not an exclusively female domain (Ball et al. 2007; Legarth et al. 2005).

In line with Continuity Theory, gender roles and responsibilities are likely to remain intact following retirement. Thus, if stereotypically gendered activity patterns have been experienced up to retirement then are they likely to continue into retirement? Elsewhere it has been recognised that the retirement of one half of a couple may positively or negatively affect the relationship dynamic, for example, blurring of roles within the home and the relationship (Barnes and Parry 2004; Davey & Szinovacz 2004; Kim & Moen 2001; Kulik 2001; Kulik 2002; Pienta 2003). This might lead to an enhanced relationship due to more equal use of time and responsibilities or, conversely, this can result in conflict due to a perceived intrusion into the role and routine of the partner.

Pause point

Reflective case study

David and June have been married for 40 years. During their marriage they have taken on stereotyped gender roles. David worked full-time and defined himself as the 'bread winner' for his family. June's main role was homemaker and mother to the couple's two sons. Since retirement, David and June have experienced conflict. David has developed an interest in cooking and enjoys spending time in the kitchen. June is unhappy with this as she is used to planning and preparing family meals. However,

David is unhappy when June asks him for help with household chores, e.g. cleaning, ironing, etc. as he sees this as her role as homemaker. June argues that David should share these chores now that he no longer goes out to work.

Reflect on this family dynamic:

Which gender stereotypes are demonstrated by David and June?

Do you think that either of them is justified in their frustration with the other? Have you experienced similar conflict yourself or observed them in others?

If you were working with this couple, how would you facilitate a discussion between David and June about issues raised, and how would you enable them to move forward?

Record what knowledge and skills you may need to effectively facilitate such a sensitive discussion. Also, note and recognise the personal and professional skills and knowledge you may already possess.

The activities with which people engage following retirement depend on the individual and their tastes and values. However, certain trends can be observed between populations. The most obvious gender difference is that many women currently in the ageing population gave up employment when their first child was born. Although they might have had career plans, to an extent society expected them to be full-time mothers and there was no maternity leave legislation in place in the United Kingdom at that time. Many men in this generation, however, report different pressures, mainly securing employment that would enable them to provide financially for their families.

Differences in employment history between men and women can have a great impact on attitudes to retirement. After more than four decades of employment, many ageing men report being happy to retire. Many women in this population, however, can be more reluctant to cease working as their careers were fragmented by childcare and family responsibilities. Stereotypical gender roles can also be demonstrated in the choice of activities in which individuals may engage following retirement, with men possibly concentrating on household maintenance and decorating, while women prioritise more domestic tasks. Furthermore, there are often marked differences in the leisure activity choices between genders. Ball et al. (2007) describe a study in which they explored the attitudes of healthy ageing adults regarding participation in leisure activities. Results suggest that leisure was organised into four categories (active leisure, passive leisure, hobbies and interests, other leisure activities e.g. travel), with marked gender differences, as more men participated in active leisure while more women enjoyed hobbies and interests. In support of Bowling (2008), this study also found that more passive activity, such as reading, became more pronounced with age. The perceived benefits varied between individuals and illustrate once again the subjective nature of meaningful activity.

A similar study to that conducted by Ball et al. (2007) was carried out by Legarth et al. (2005) in which the views of Danish ageing adults were explored regarding meaningful activities. The results demonstrated similarities with those of Ball et al. (2007), and although the activities recorded were varied, once again men preferred the more physical activities while more women preferred domestic crafts. This result is interesting as gender roles seem to be pronounced within this age cohort, even though the studies sampled populations in different countries thus supporting a cross-cultural dimension.

Pause point

Think about gender stereotypes:

Do you think society still conforms to these?

Have you ever made a choice based on society's expectation for your gender, such as a career choice or activity choice?

If so, what would have been the consequence of a different decision?

Record some of your own thoughts on issues raised above. Reflect on potential ethical issues that may arise from modern day professional practice.

Historically, Fairhurst (2003) commented that research into the retirement transition mainly focussed on the experiences of men, as these are the individuals that have been perceived to be mostly affected by retirement due to the cessation of employment. However, she recognises that "wider research is required due to changing social conventions, such as increased numbers of females in the workforce, but also due to the understanding that retirement of one partner can affect the quality of life of the other" (pp. 31–33).

One of the studies that considers how men and women adjust to retirement was carried out by Barnes and Parry (2004) as part of a wider initiative for the Joseph Rowntree Foundation. The findings suggest that gender roles in married couples often become more fluid following retirement, especially if one spouse remains in work. Also, the transition for women who worked was found to be smoother as women tended to consider family duties as a main priority throughout their lives while men often focussed on career and financial obligations. Although Barnes and Parry (2004) found that "marriage has a positive effect upon retirement satisfaction" (p .227), they also recognised that single people tend to develop wider social networks to maintain social contacts in later life. They conclude with the general finding that "in retirement, as throughout the life-course, men and women occupy various gendered identities that are mediated by class and ethnicity" (p. 229). As a result, this study, although focussing on gender roles and marital status, again reinforces the subjective nature of human experience and the heterogeneity of the ageing population. This study also reflects the tenets of Continuity Theory, suggesting that there is continuity of gendered roles both during and after the retirement transition process.

It is important to remember that as the ageing population is increasing in number it is also developing an increased diversity and societal acceptance of difference. As such, retirement does not only impact upon the lives of heterosexual married couples, as in most contemporary households, family units are not homogeneous, and may include same-sex couples as well as those who are widowed, divorced, remarried, never married or transgender.

Lesbian, gay, bisexual and transgender ageing (LGBT)

Positively, in the United Kingdom and other parts of the Western world, same-sex couples are experiencing a level of acceptance and appreciation never seen before. Although this is clearly not reflected by the views of all citizens, from the Sexual Offences Act 1967 to the Marriage (Same Sex Couples) Act 2013, LGBT individuals are now acknowledged by a plethora of legislation that aims to offer equality and protection to this sector of the population. Acceptance may have brought with it a level of confidence to more fully integrate into aspects of life denied to this community in years gone by. Such integration may include open participation and access to a wider spectrum of social and activity groups amongst the general population.

LGBT ageing adults may positively and at times negatively experience unique economic and health disparities. They may disproportionately be affected by loneliness, stigma, and mental health conditions due to a lifetime of unique stressors associated with being in a minority group. It is important to recognise that they may still face dual discrimination due to their age and their sexual orientation or gender identity. Social isolation is also a concern because LGBT ageing adults are more likely to live alone, more likely to be single and less likely to have children than their heterosexual counterparts. All of these considerations can be compounded by intersections of sex, race, ethnicity and disability.

The impact of gender stereotypes as discussed above may not so easily be applied to same-sex couples as they may not conform to the reductive viewpoint that one will automatically adopt a particular role.

As with many heterosexual couples, whether married or not, the roles adopted may rely more on individual choice and interest, rather than solely on societal expectations. As such, one member of a same-sex couple might well take on the role of homemaker and engage in the expected activities, such as cooking and cleaning while the partner may take on a different role. In such cases it is reasonable to suggest that their experience of retirement might include the conflict and role blurring experienced by heterosexual couples. However, potentially, there exist more opportunities now for LGBT individuals to make a positive transition into retirement due to the increased ability to engage in activities that will offer them optimum involvement and well-being, due to enhanced legal protections and societal acceptance.

From an occupational engagement perspective, irrespective of gender, marital status or sexual orientation, volunteering can and appears to be an important mechanism for ageing adults to meet new people, reduce social isolation and extend connections. The choice of meaningful occupations in retirement can be influenced by so many, and often complex, personal factors. Such factors include finance, health, environment, and even the differing opportunities in relation to living in a more rural environment as opposed to a more urban one. It may be difficult to focus on one generic meaningful retirement occupation that applies to all, irrespective of gender, sexuality, culture and age. This said, volunteering and different levels of engagement in it seems to cross all borders and generations. It is argued that many charity shops, luncheon clubs and social events would be compromised if it was not for the dedication of primarily ageing adults who service and run such ventures.

Volunteering

Volunteering is a significant and meaningful occupation for community-minded citizens. A volunteer is defined as an individual who is usually unpaid, who participates by choice through an intermediary body, organisation, group or community and who provides direct services for another's benefit, often including a role in caring for others. In the United Kingdom, it is not by any means a minority activity. Moreover, a substantial proportion of non-profit groups rely on volunteers, often ageing adults, to realise their objectives.

Whilst there are undoubtedly many social opportunities for ageing adults in which to interact, volunteering is able to provide a valuable and much broader, more diverse network of interactions such as other colleagues, clients and host organisations. One of the other positive benefits of volunteering is the scope for ageing adults to engage in physical activities, to experience themselves in productive roles and to increase social interactions and contacts. Effective volunteer programmes can be designed for ageing adults so that they can contribute to successful ageing, ensuring that they are viewed as a skilled, valuable untapped resource

Ageing adults, as they transition into retirement, may seek to fill a void by offering their skills, knowledge and interest to a wide variety of community groups and charitable organisations. Such a role may offer benefits in terms of social capital they accrue via their citizenship activities. Volunteering can also further enhance occupational skills and knowledge. It is clear that volunteering has great potential for better health and personal happiness and there can clearly be a correlation between volunteering and life satisfaction, contentment, well-being, self-esteem, physical, mental, emotional and spiritual health. Participation in such meaningful occupation may well help ageing adults to flourish.

It has been suggested by Pettican and Prior (2011, p. 18) that the "close and multifaceted relationships between occupational engagement and the maintenance of health and well-being for individuals is intertwined and connected substantially in sustaining well-being". Social structure may therefore allow socialisation which can include the community, family, voluntary groups, peers or friends. Keeping friendships and relationships in this way will boost well-being and can contribute significantly to the prevention of physical and psychological decline as a way to aid successful ageing and maintain or improve welfare and health. Socialising within a voluntary context will be fundamental to benefit and support well-being and happiness. Suggested benefits to socialising in this way will include opportunities to meet new people, meet with friends and experience new opportunities, to maintain or learn new skills. Many positive factors to socialising through engagement in occupations have clearly been identified but barriers have also been highlighted. Suggested barriers can be environmental issues including rural locations and transport limitations. Finances, time, commitments, loss of friends or relocating can also be issues for ageing adults. Biological barriers can also prevent the ageing adult from socialising due to health issues; these can be physical or psychological factors that may be associated with this age group and are identified as functional or mobility issues, illness or disease. This said, many ageing adults are skilled at managing such barriers to enable socialisation with others within the community and family to maximise fulfilment and well-being.

Pause point and case study

Marilyn is a 67-year-old lady who gave up her paid employment as a shop assistant because of a long history of alcohol abuse and some mobility difficulties. She has received some professional support to overcome her alcohol abuse and subsequent depression and is now able to control her social drinking. She has become socially isolated as her coping mechanism for controlling her drinking has been to withdraw completely from her friends in the local social club. She is now fearing that she will return to drinking excessively alone at home as a way of coping. In talking to you she is expressing a desire to work in the local charity shop, and to start making contact with her friends again.

> How would you go about supporting Marilyn in her current situation?

> How may you enable Marilyn to prioritise her goals? What themes might you raise for Marilyn?

How would you go about planting a seed for Marilyn to consider volunteering as a meaningful occupation?

Return to the 4 D Model in Chapter 2 and try and apply it as a framework to working with Marilyn.

Once you have done this:

What are your key learning points?

Does working with the 4 D Model help you? If not, outline the reasons?

What opportunities and challenges does the 4 D model offer you in this context? Does the 4 D Model offer opportunities and challenges for Marilyn?

Record your analysis and make some notes on how useful this has been for you.

This chapter has briefly considered important themes such as gender, marital status and sexuality in terms of occupational engagement in retirement. As one example of an occupation where gender, marital status or sexual orientation may be of no significance in terms of contribution and stereotypical prejudice, the benefits of volunteering has been introduced as an example with a focus on how socialisation can support the maintenance of well-being and happiness. Highlighting the importance of engagement through socialisation may demonstrate the value such occupations may potentially have on lowering levels of psychological distress and elevating levels of well-being and life satisfaction.

The following chapter will introduce the concept of mindfulness as a way to address potential distress. Applying mindfulness skills to retirement coaching may allow the professional to consider and explore how this can be used to facilitate creative, independent lifestyle redesign in preparation for, and following retirement.

CHAPTER 5

MINDFULNESS AND LIFESTYLE REDESIGN IN AGEING ADULTS

"To see a persons' specialities rather than their weaknesses is an act of co-operation."
Brahma Kumaris

This chapter will introduce the concept of mindfulness. There is growing evidence that mindfulness is effective in lowering levels of psychological distress and elevating levels of well-being and life satisfaction. In the context of ageing adults and transitional retirement this chapter will introduce the concept of mindfulness in a way that relates to the professional health and social care worker and their role as a retirement coach. Its application in practice has the potential to encourage such professionals and coaches to achieve mindfulness in a way that engages what is referred to in Chapters 6 and 7 as 'the appreciative eye' – a more positive vision and approach to ageing. Seeing ageing adults through such a lens can well encourage the development of a more person-centred, relational and empathic approach to supporting ageing adults. The United Kingdom Mental Health Foundations' report on Mindfulness (2010) states how mindfulness practice can help the individual to become more aware of their thoughts and feelings, less enmeshed in them and able to manage and include them.

Appreciating mindfulness in practice

The last twenty years has seen a significant shift in focus and appreciation of mindfulness, its popularity encouraged by increasing research evidence of its effective impact on mental health and well-being. Its full impact as a potential and effective low- cost intervention to stress, growing sickness rates in the public sector along with increasing absence from work makes it a skill base that can, with professional training and education, benefit a wide spectrum of society including ageing adults entering transitional retirement. The interim report of the United Kingdom Mindfulness All-Party Parliamentary Group (MAPPG) (The Mindful Initiative 2014 p. 1) states: "This country is facing a major mental health crisis, with growing effects of depression, anxiety and stress … The economic impact of poor mental health is estimated to be £100 billion in the UK …"

What is mindfulness?

Siegel (2007 p. 5) sees mindfulness as "a waking up from life on automatic", a definition which certainly applies in modern day culture as more and more people exist with the consequences of stress on auto-pilot in high-pressure work environments. Mindfulness is not by any means a new approach. Kabat-Zinn as far back as 1994 (p. 180) defined mindfulness as "the awareness that emerges through paying attention on purpose, in the present moment, and non-judgmentally to the unfolding of experience moment by moment." The practice of mindfulness encourages both the retirement coach and the ageing adult alike to awaken to embrace a reflective and more relational partnership. A mindful professional and a retirement coach will potentially develop a more open mind and not be caught in, or default to, an evaluative and analytical way of thinking. When applied by the ageing adult, Langer (1989) reminds us that one of the simplest and most natural methods of reducing self-evaluation and criticism is to assume a mindset of mindfulness rather than mindlessness.

The mindful retirement coach

Mindfulness offers "the ability to quiet and still our minds, ending impulsivity and silence the voice of the inner critic and judge" (Roberts and Machon 2015 p. 85). They further affirm how "Mindfulness is the capacity to be attentive and aware without the compulsion to analyse or solve" (p. 86). Mindfulness therefore enables the retirement coach to be fully present and free from distraction, in order to more fully attend their client. This permits them to be more fully in the moment, alert yet relaxed, reflective and relational and able to respond to the ageing adult as their client and the coaching conversation. Such skills can cultivate an attitude and an approach that is non-judgmental. The ageing adult in turn will experience the presence of unconditional positive regard. This highlights a capacity to accept without condition, the presence of the coach is devoid of the compulsion to critically judge the ageing adult and instead, can fully enable. If the professional and retirement coach can be consciously mindful, then they have the potential to create a valuable space where observation and self-discovery becomes the norm, allowing meaningful and thoughtful relationship and dialogue to emerge.

When reflecting on the role of the mindful retirement coach, it is important to focus on the present moment, possibility and potential and not to feel compelled to be drawn into the emotions and thoughts from the past. Dane (2011) also affirms that for him, mindfulness is a state of consciousness in which attention is focussed more on the present moment. It is clear from the literature that mindfulness is believed to be strongly aligned to fostering relationships, a connection with the other. Through the retirement coach practising mindfulness, fostering appreciation and enabling the ageing adult to expand their field of conscious awareness, there comes the prospect of developing true insight. In turn this will provide a helpful platform for the retirement coach to equally and simultaneously become more attuned to the thoughts and feelings of the ageing adult.

When offering a professional retirement coaching experience, practising mindfulness will bring along with it a valuable depth and breadth to a capacity to support and enable. In essence, what one learns to do is to develop the capacity to reflect on one's own experience and that of the ageing adult. As part of the practising tool kit, mindfulness offers a way to discover more valuable information about the ageing adult and about oneself. In sharing such awareness and empathy the ageing adult is encouraged to include and integrate valuable experiences, thoughts and feelings into the process. This helps create a much more holistic picture and shared reality and to then agree the most authentic response (Roberts and Machon 2015).

Mindfulness and improved perception

Practising mindfulness is a way to improve perception of one's self and others. Its application in practice suggests that this approach promises to be highly beneficial for individual personal and professional continuing development. Claxton (2004) talks about the 'cultivation of mindfulness', and describes its potential benefits in the following way (p. 221): "In this state of sharp awareness of experience at a low level of interpretation, three phenomenal effects occur. First the 'world' seems clearer, cleaner and more objective; less, to use Hermann Hesse's phrase, 'a cloudy mirror of our own desire'. Second, assumptions and projections which have previously been dissolved surreptitiously in perception now become visible in their own right. They operate, if they still continue to do so, 'downstream' of the moment of conscious perception, on the surface, rather than upstream, invisibly. And third, the mingling of cognitive currents that extended processing allows, is freed of the narrowing concerns of self- reference: it is firmly channelled by consideration of personal advantage and disadvantage and 'creativity' becomes more playful and unbounded."

Mindfulness, when applied by a retirement coach in practice, is therefore about keeping the attention on more immediate, less elaborated state, using Bachkirova's (2011 p. 184) example of "noticing the sensation in your hands when you do the washing up, watching and listening to the water running … If we do not share this sensation with the narrator, it does not hijack the attention into creating another story of the self washing the dishes".

Improved perception, therefore, is a precious and valuable asset and a gift that should be valued by both the retirement coach and ageing adult. The cultivation of mindfulness can forge a close and meaningful, purposeful and perceptive relationship between both parties.

Pause point

When reflecting on the potential benefits of mindfulness:

What, in your opinion, are the key implications for the ageing adult and the retirement coach alike, when a more perceptive and relational dialogue occurs?

Record any continuing professional development needs you may have in relation to achieve a better understanding of mindfulness and its potential application in practice. Create a development plan as a way to fulfil your needs.

Improved reflection and empathy

The capacity of the retirement coach to aspire to be fully reflective and empathic rather than impulsive, offers the individual the opportunity to extend their outlook, perception and conscious awareness. The professional as a coach will be able to look clearly through a particular lens, and as a result gather information that will be more accurate and real, seeing a picture of current reality that can be more in service of the ageing adult. Such an approach can be seen as a platform to allow the retirement coach to be fully relational with the ageing adult in a way that assists the individual to express their respective strengths and also, when they choose, their vulnerability. Being able to support and coach in such an open-minded way, accommodating the ageing adults' subjective experience will be beneficial. This provides an opportunity to explore what strengths and positive attributes the ageing adult wish to bring to life and their chosen occupation. This openness creates the opportunity for the ageing adult to speak of their vulnerability and fear and what may otherwise limit. A reflective retirement coach will be able to work more empathically when engaging and fully including the ageing adult because they are less objectified and potentially seen as a whole person beyond the focus of their capabilities and life stage.

Pause point

How may you move to a place of true empathy with an ageing adult?

What resources may you need to call upon?

When will you know that the ageing adult feels attended to?

Reflect and record your learning.

Being responsive

Being responsive in an unconditional and empathic manner can be key for success in the retirement coach–ageing adult relationship. Key characteristics and implications of an attentive and responsive retirement coach will enable the individual to demonstrate complete acceptance and non-judgement of the ageing adult as a client and as a person. The retirement coach can show that they have the capacity to give their full attention to the ageing adult, demonstrate unconditional positive regard and so offer a totally accepting and non-judgemental attitude to the content of the coaching session. Such capacity can build awareness and attentiveness and fosters the capacity of the coach to listen more intently (Roberts and Machon 2015). In turn, the ageing adult will experience the coach's growing presence, resulting in an invitation to be more visible and fully seen and importantly, listened to and heard. Achieving this will lead to the expansion of the feeling of trust and safety, allowing the ageing adult the opportunity to work more openly and deeply on their transitional journey.

Pause point

Do you consider yourself to be good at developing and offering unconditional positive regard?

How do you strengthen your unconditional positive regard rather than feel compelled to judge feelings or someone's position?

When you potentially find yourself in a place of conscious or unconscious judgement, no matter how big or small, make notes on how you might get to a place where you become fully responsive as a way to work with those feelings?

Might there be any learning resources you can identify that may allow you to get to a more confident place on this matter?

Building active client engagement, motivation and resourcefulness

Aligning personal values, beliefs and purpose will be an important factor in transitional retirement. The retirement coach will need to engage and empower the ageing adult to consider what specific resources they can access and bring to their own plan of action. Approaching coaching conversations in this way will offer the individual the ability to redefine their choices as opportunities in times of adversity and so is likely to help build personal resilience.

Bringing compassion to practice

Most of the world's major traditions advocate compassion and kind orientation to others. Commonly, compassion is defined as "being sensitive to the suffering of self and others with a deep commitment to try and prevent and relive it" (Gilbert 2014 p. 1). What is important about developing compassion is to gain the ability to engage supportively and wisely with what is often painful and to seek to understand its roots. Compassion is not about being overwhelmed by one's own or other's challenges or pain; it is about being superficially attentive, approachable and kind as a way to connect. Central to compassion is tuning in to the nature of 'being stuck' and the subsequent and potential suffering which may emerge. Compassion is about understanding to the depth of one's very being, and to see clearly into its source; but "equally important is to be committed to relieve it and to rejoice in the possibility of the alleviation of suffering for all" (Gilbert 2014 p. 3).

Working with true empathy is to model compassion in coaching practice. The retirement coach's capacity to offer empathy and yet be able to detach and reflect allows the practitioner to work with an objective intimacy (Roberts and Machon 2015). This quality ensures a deeply caring approach in coaching without the professional becoming overly attached or showing an unhealthy dependency.

Being person-centred

A mindful, person-centred retirement coach has the capacity to view the ageing adult holistically, as a whole person and to consider how their emotional, psychological, physical, mental, spiritual and social needs will be met as key elements of the transition process. The innate value and humanity of the ageing adult can be recognised by the coach who can model working with integrity, compassion, respect and dignity in practice.

When the mindful retirement coach can genuinely work in partnership with the ageing adult, they may be empowered to engage in all decisions pertaining to transitional retirement and this may be seen as central to a trusting coaching relationship. The ageing adult is an equal partner who is in the driving seat at all times and actively engaged in defining and agreeing the way forward. The retirement coach will be empowered to work extremely flexibly, offering qualitative and quantitative aspects of support dependent on need. What also develops is a social conscience that enables a more collaborative approach to care as a true partnership initiative. Collectively, what is realised in practice is responsive person-centred attention and care (Roberts and Machon 2015). When a retirement coach can show an appreciation of the ageing adults' current life situation as they transition into retirement, including their family and home environment, and their personal preferences and experiences, then coaching will be more closely aligned with an individual's values and so engages the retiree more fully. Working in partnership with the ageing adult will result in more effective and affirmative decisions from complete and unbiased information when assessing, for example, a range of occupational choices. This type of coaching is likely to foster a culture of co-creation. The retirement coach demonstrates trust, empathy, respect, compassion and dignity; these qualities are the foundations of responsive person- centred coaching. What is co-created are meaningful relationships that are genuine partnerships built upon effective communication (Roberts and Machon 2015). Responsive person-centred retirement coaching will enhance the importance of collaborative working. In this way the coach will ensure intervention and support together to be user-focussed and deliver guidance that is mindful of individual need and abilities, preferences, lifestyles and personal goals. This enables control and empowerment back to the ageing adult and their family and wider network. It also aids to promote independence and full engagement in occupational choice, health and well-being and transitional retirement.

There are two interdependent psychologies that make up kindness and compassion. The first is the psychology that enables the coach to be empowered and motivated to engage with the ageing adults' potential challenges in the form of pain or suffering (emotional, physical, psychological or spiritual), and to attend to it in a non-judgmental way. The second will enable the coach to work skilfully and carefully toward the alleviation and prevention of that suffering and its causes, for example, a reduction in income, grief or loss. Succeeding in this way will allow the process to be contextualised in an approach that is mindful, observant, and familiar with the situation (Gilbert 2014).

Pause point and case study

Alison, who recently retired from the manufacturing industry, has been working with a retirement coach for two months. Last week she was diagnosed with bowel cancer and has spoken to you at length about its impact on herself and her family.

What coaching skills would be useful to Alison in your conversations?

How might you demonstrate some of these – including listening, empathy and unconditional positive regard?

What would enable you to have coaching conversations of this nature?

How might Alison be motivated through this experience? How would you demonstrate your sensitivity towards her? How might you empathise with her?

In this scenario, you may consider that interacting in this way may support both wisdom and courage. Do you think that human behaviour may be key to the continuing development of the abilities and skills required to alleviate and prevent suffering? Might working at this level show true caring? Record what skills you require to enable you to take an interest in the overall well-being of the ageing adult you may be working with.

Mindful potential

A wide variety of health and social care professionals including those who develop coaching skills are beginning to explore ways to increase mindfulness in their practice. Interestingly, current research does not indicate that professionals' self-reported mindfulness enhances client outcomes, and it is clear that better measures of mindfulness will need to be developed or different research designs that do not rely on self-report measures will need to be explored. Garland and Gaylord (2009) propose that mindfulness research should encompass four domains, namely performance-based measures of mindfulness, as opposed to self-reports, scientific evaluation of notions espoused by Buddhist traditions, neuro-imaging technology to verify self-report data and changes in gene expression as a result of mindfulness. Research along these lines will be more likely to enhance one's understanding of mindfulness and its potential benefits to areas such as retirement coaching, counselling and psychotherapy.

In summary, having briefly explored the nature of reactive, relational and responsive care, if one were to consider these three aspects of retirement coaching more as a continuum and less as three distinct perspectives, it would ensure full inclusion and participation of the ageing adult in the design and implementation of their transitional retirement plan. The retirement coach is in a privileged position to enable and empower the ageing adult to identify and realise choices and desired outcomes that align with their own personal values, beliefs, aspirations and purpose. The coach can be an invaluable resource to enable and empower the ageing adult to harness their motivation and their own resourcefulness in support of their health, well-being and occupational engagement. Subsequent chapters will explore further how opening the 'appreciative eye', offering a more appreciative vision of self and others, can be a vital step in awakening to relational and empathic coaching and that mindfulness in daily practice can allow the professional as a retirement coach to maximise on their own full personal and professional potential.

CHAPTER 6

APPRECIATIVE INQUIRY – HEALTH AND WELL-BEING THROUGH OCCUPATION

This chapter provides a deeper insight into how appreciative inquiry will help to motivate and empower ageing adults, communities and groups to change their perspectives on life, occupations and situations such as retirement. This will be achieved by adapting the 4 D Model of practice described in Chapter 2 and applying it to short case studies as in Chapters 2 and 4, This chapter further guides ageing adults, retirement coaches and supportive health and social care professionals on ways to embrace and promote a more positive, respectful, compassionate and dignified approach to ageing and retirement. For these reasons, appreciative inquiry and the application of what will be referred to here as the 'appreciative eye' (explored further in Chapter 7) has the potential to be widely used as a means of enhancing and affirming quality of life and well-being for professionals and ageing adults. By encouraging openness and negotiation among people in this context, this methodology will support attempts to give collective and community-wide ownership and authorship of positive transformation. It provides a procedure in which affirmative dialogue and reflection becomes a collaborative means of improving systems. It aspires to be a process of negotiation, and as such it is not imposed, due to its person-centred focus. Therefore, consequent changes are more likely to be accepted by ageing adults since they have been proactive in evaluating themselves and their aspirations for a satisfying transition into retirement and beyond.

The primary aim of introducing appreciative inquiry as an approach is important for a variety of reasons and for a wide spectrum of different people. It has the potential to empower individuals and communities to influence what appears at times to be an over emphasis on seeing old age and retirement as a problem, a barrier, a burden and a challenge. Instead, seeing the world with an appreciative eye has the capacity to view growing old and retirement as an opportunity, by seeing potential, aiming for the very best, creating and sustaining the energy needed to act into a more positively envisioned future. Working with it in partnership with ageing adults is an exciting consideration and one that can positively impact on how individuals make the transition into retirement in a much more affirmative manner. Its potential will create a new foundation for enabling positive, transformative change in how individuals perceive their own transition and how professional facilitation and life coaching can assist those ageing adults to manage change.

Applying appreciative inquiry to transitional retirement

Applying the principles of appreciative inquiry in this context simply means looking and focussing primarily at the affirmative opportunities for ageing adults who are in the process of transitioning into retirement and seeing and appreciating all that is good about this life stage and the opportunities afforded to ageing adults as they retire. Such a vision is positive, exciting and life changing. Rather than seeing retirement, and indeed old age, as a problem, appreciative inquiry is applied by ageing adults to encourage a more positive self-perspective in the context of transitional retirement. Importantly, it can also guide professional health, social care and support workers applying coaching skills to their practice to challenge potential negative or preconceived mindsets or beliefs about this life stage and event. The idea of using the lens of the appreciative eye assumes that in every aspect of life something works (Roberts and Machon 2015), and as such, appreciative inquiry can open up the context in which some negative and problematic perspectives can be changed or balanced as a way to introduce the probability of a much more affirmative and creative outlook on ageing adults and their lives. This paradox seeks to marry both the **'can't do'** and the **'can do'** concepts in an approach and process that harnesses the strengths of both through a more comprehensive consideration of that which serves and that which limits ageing adults' lives. This paradox mirrors one's deepest understanding of human nature since it views the ageing adult to be in a continuous process of becoming, emerging and growing as well as seeing the individual as a problem to be solved – dealing with what is. The paradoxical approach also mirrors one's deepest understanding of human nature since it views ageing adults as people with some challenges and problems who are in a process of becoming. This approach considers both what is and also what will be. A negative preconceived idea about ageing adults as retirees will devalue some peoples' understanding of human nature by judging them as a problem needing to be solved. This is often overly portrayed in some media coverage of growing old. If society and the media see an ageing adult only as a problem (what they cannot do) they become blind to their full human potential (what they can do) and what they may become and what invaluable contribution they continue to make to society during this life stage. The intention is to apply this notion to ageing adults and transitional retirement.

Appreciative inquiry suggests that ageing adults as retirees not only acknowledge any potential challenges and problems, but also look for exciting new opportunities, new projects, flexibility of time with significant others, and the expansion of social networks. The tangible result of the inquiry process is a series of statements that describe where the ageing adult wants to be, based on the high moments of where they have been in both their personal and professional (such as paid employment) lives. The same notion will apply to the retirement coach's continuous personal and professional development experience. Because the appreciative statements are grounded in real experiences and history, ageing adults will know how to repeat their success. The idea, therefore, in planning and engaging in transitional retirement is to approach prospective challenges with an appreciative eye and less with a negative and potential analytical eye (described in Chapter 7). By seeing the world through an appreciative lens, it may help to cultivate and put into perspective an analytical eye which seeks to identify problems and determine their possible solution. An appreciative process has the potential to encourage the unfolding of innovation and creativity in this context (Machon, 2010). Professionals who approach ageing adults with a more analytical, problem-focussed eye may be limiting their own full potential to be truly person-centred. Working with the appreciative eye, professionals as retirement coaches can facilitate ageing adults to look at the transition with a more positive outlook. What is apparent here is that ageing adults can expand the capacity of their thinking by opening an appreciative eye with the use of a rational and critical intellect. The appreciative eye in this context is described as looking at a situation or scenario with an empathetic, positive and holistic view. The opening of the appreciative eye parallels that what one might term as the opening of the heart, a more compassionate focus (Roberts and Machon 2015). What will emerge is the development of a level of thinking where ageing adults and professionals alike shift from just seeing problems to view the living individual as themselves. In this context the role of the professional as a retirement coach becomes central in enabling this to happen throughout the transitional experience. The appreciative eye can define a recipe for success by helping the ageing adult to consider previous experience and to reuse positive outcomes. As such, this approach acknowledges the importance of the influence of life course events on present day decision-making, as described by Continuity Theory in previous chapters of this book. Professionals as retirement coaches can therefore facilitate a positive approach to ensure ageing adults engage themselves in the transitional process and to use such transferable skills in practice.

Appreciative inquiry in practice – asking the appropriate questions

The key for success when applying appreciative inquiry is to offer the right and most affirmative questions. Instead of asking ageing adults, for example, 'what challenges do you now face in retirement?' how would it be if the first question was 'what opportunities does retirement now give you?' or, 'what exciting projects you do have planned?' With this in mind, choosing occupations of choice will be the most critical step in applying appreciative inquiry as ageing adults move towards and into retirement. What occupations ageing adults choose to engage with will become their reality and therefore it is important to consider the most appropriate and engaging for each individual.

Pause point

When working with, or interviewing an ageing person during this transition:

> What questions might you ask a retiree to find out what worked well in the past and what works well in the present?

> What positive aspects may now be influencing the future?

> Make a list of the questions and reflect on what response you might get. Since appreciative inquiry is a generative process, attempt to create your own affirmative questions that you could ask an ageing adult in this situation. Create some provocative propositions in order to positively keep the best at a conscious level. As they are symbolic statements, be aware that they may have from stories that actually took place in the lives of these individuals, groups or communities. Grounding in reality, be it history, tradition and facts, will distinguish appreciative inquiry from other visioning methods in which dreams and aspirations serve as the primary basis for the vision. For the future, ask the individual – what is their potential for success in the future – the aspirations and exciting plans of the individual. Do they have any wishes or longings?

> Appreciative inquiry will encourage one to assume that each ageing adult's challenge is in the process of becoming something more than its current state, that the pathway to discover this potential is to initially identify and place emphasis on what is working well. It is not only what works well currently, but also what the individual might potentially wish to achieve in the future. This intervention embraces strengths, potentiality and aspirations, assuming that success can be repeated. Seeing through the lens of the appreciative eye will achieve sustainable, creative and transformative change in one's personal life and in professional practice.

Pause point for the ageing adults

Looking at your past, what affirmative skills are you bringing forward to retirement?

What excites you about your current situation?

Looking through an appreciative lens, what advice would you give a colleague or a friend who is about to enter the transition into retirement?

List the 10 best things about retirement? (more if you choose to)

How easy was it for you to remain focused on the positive aspects without first thinking about the negatives?

Record and share your thoughts with someone if you feel confident to do so. Observe their reaction!

What does appreciative inquiry envisage

Appreciative inquiry assumes that a positive experience comes from collaborative is working well for the ageing adult. From an occupational perspective, it can be essential to move away from seeing transitional retirement through eyes which seek what is broken and needs to be fixed, to a place of understanding appreciative inquiry as a process to guide both professionals and ageing adults to focus on the very best of what is and what works well. When effectively applied, appreciative inquiry can enhance individuals to share in the discovery of the source of yet unrealised self- potential, growth and continuous personal development. Introducing appreciative inquiry as an added dimension to professional support of ageing adults invites retirement coaches to engage more fully, and on a different and more positive level. Ageing adults in turn are invited to do the same within their own social and personal networks in an effort to explore each other's successes, their emotions and future aspirations. Continuing to learn about themselves and contemplate more deeply how to overcome challenges in this manner will become an important element in the health and well-being debate.

Challenging the appreciative inquiry 4 D Model

One important challenge when applying the principles of appreciative inquiry as a technique is the language and terminology used to frame it. Words such as discovery, dreams, design and destiny, as used in Cooperrider's original 4 D model, can in cultural terms appear unscientific and open to interpretation. Making sense of appreciative inquiry language becomes a challenge in itself and will need to be addressed by those who choose to build on its potential in coaching. Appreciative inquiry is by its own nature an expansive, relational and empathic relational approach. Language is important in terms of acceptance, and professionals as retirement coaches and ageing adults alike will need to discuss alternative terms that will be more acceptable and better understood. This challenge can be seen as an opportunity to introduce the concept of appreciative inquiry to retirement coaches, and to request that they seek to define a language and terminology that is more fitting to transitional retirement when working with ageing adults.

In summary, this chapter has highlighted the paradox that appreciative inquiry, in the context of health and well-being through occupation, can embrace both the individuals' being and becoming. Gathering a wide spectrum of information from the ageing adult will provide a more complete picture of their will, their dreams, and their motivations. It attempts to respect the innate paradoxical nature of the ageing adult and considers both their current state and future aspirations.

It emerges that appreciative inquiry can speak to the co-evolutionary search for the best in people, their communities and the relevant world around them. In its broadest sense, it involves systematic discovery of what gives 'life' to individuals when they are most alive, most effective, and most constructively capable in economic, ecological, and human terms. In essence, appreciative inquiry involves the arts, science and the practice of asking questions that strengthen a system's capacity to apprehend, anticipate, and heighten positive human potential. It centrally involves the effective application of inquiry through the crafting of the 'unconditional positive question'. Appreciative inquiry encourages the opening of the imagination and innovation, it seeks to build a constructive bond between people and the massive entirety of what they talk and reminisce about: achievements, recognition, successes, assets, unexplored potentials, innovations, strengths, opportunities, high point moments, insights, lived values, traditions, stories, expressions of wisdom and visions of valued and possible futures.

So how might such paradox inform and evolve one's approach to ageing and its relationship with transitional retirement? Can this paradox illuminate one's understanding of envisaged problems and problem solving in this context? Giving such attention to the retirees of today and those of tomorrow may offer the rare opportunity for discussion of limitations as well as strengths. Such openness can be the key that will unlock the occupational potential of tomorrow.

With this in mind, Chapter 7 introduces a new and innovative model of practice for professionals working with ageing adults. The 3 Eye Model has evolved from work and research undertaken in the health and social care sector in the United Kingdom and has been heavily influenced by appreciative inquiry and the 4 D Model as developed by Cooperrider and Whitney (2000). The 3 Eye Model in its original form was researched and developed by Roberts and Machon (2015) in response to the recommendations of the Francis report (2013) and is seen as a new creative and innovative model of practice. This model in the context of this book has been adapted from its original application in health and social care practice to that of retirement coaching with ageing adults and transitional retirement.

CHAPTER 7

PERSON-CENTRED TRANSITIONAL RETIREMENT COACHING

"We are here to do,
and through doing to learn;
and through learning to know;
and through knowing to experience wonder;
and through wonder to attain wisdom;
and through wisdom to find simplicity;
and through simplicity to give attention;
and through attention to see what needs to be done."

Rabbi Ben Hei Hei

This chapter will introduce the value of developing more of a person-centred coaching opportunity for those individuals embracing the retirement process. The ability to coach is increasingly employed in professional practice in private, leisure, retirement, health and social care. Using a coaching approach as a platform allows creativity, intuition, imagination and integrity to emerge together with qualities such as compassion and dignity to inform the skills of the health and retirement coach.

In this chapter, the 3 Eye Model is brought to life as a valuable tool to remind the coach of the different ways of seeing what they can adopt in different situations. Commonly, when under stress one can appear to default to a way of working that employs the analytical eye. This defaulting behaviour and going on auto-pilot will result in a very narrow and confined vision including a preoccupation with the negative and problem solving. If the coach is to enable any client, and in this case the ageing adult, to realise their fuller potential through retirement, one is invited to learn how to expand one's vision to accommodate both the appreciative and creative eye. This process will permit the coach to create conditions of expanded awareness in which the ageing adult can work on their own solutions, foster greater resourcefulness and build their self confidence in making choices about meaningful occupations of choice.

This newly adapted and innovative 3 Eye model is explored, mindful of the work of the professional as a retirement coach. The 3 Eye Model was originally developed by Roberts and Machon (2015) and its role has already been adapted and applied to health and social care best practice and now its application is considered in terms of the work of retirement coaching and, more specifically, the ageing adult approaching transitional retirement. By applying the 3 Eye Model in a very practical way, this chapter will describe how the deployment of coaching skills and capability is key to modelling respect, encouragement, enthusiasm, compassion and dignity in working with people in later life. This chapter will describe how a coaching relationship may offer a meaningful channel through which ageing adults, groups and organisations are able to make and sustain change and build resourcefulness. This chapter will provide an insight into how those professionals can choose to incorporate this technique or framework into their current practice, for example, human resource personnel, health and social care practitioners, and those advancing their coaching skills in order to build confidence and expertise to coach and apply this to ageing adults during and after the retirement transition stage.

Deepening coaching skills can be key to optimum support for ageing adults. There are significant continuing professional development opportunities for a wide variety of health and social care professionals to develop their coaching skills. The role of life coaching, for example, is very established in corporate industry and within human resource teams across a wide variety of organisations, and more and more health and social care professionals such as occupational therapists, physiotherapists and nursing colleagues are beginning to extend their scope of practice to work as life coaches and potentially as retirement coaches. To achieve optimum skill and level of competence in coaching, most would naturally follow the necessary steps for advanced learning through a choice of coach training programmes and ultimately through accreditation with a reputable organisation that validates coaching skills and competency such as the Association of Coaches (AC) and The International Coaching Federation (ICF).

It is important to acknowledge that some ageing adults will not be able to afford to depend on some of the statutory services in the future, as predictions show that there may simply be too many retired individuals for the rest of the community to support. However, if health and social care professionals are to offer retirement coaching skills and guidance for ageing adults to make a positive transition towards occupational engagement within this life stage, individuals and support services need to understand the growing underpinning research base on the type of coaching support available.

Research has shown that the effects of transitioning into retirement can include partial identity challenges, difficulty in decision making, issues of self-trust and the search for meaningful engagement in society, critical nurturing of social relationships and self- actualisation (Osborne 2012). He states that "some aspects of preretirement life can be predictive of a successful transition" (Osborne 2012 p. 45).

The retirement coach as a facilitator and enabler

As professionals utilising coaching skills, it is the development of a mutual and trusting relationship between themselves and the ageing person which is key. It is designed to build trust and to create the conditions for the individual to do their real and important work in coaching, in order to help the individual to determine their own destiny as they transit into change, retirement and beyond. Retirement coaching enables and facilitates such change and narrows the gap between where an ageing adult is in their life and where ideally, they would like to be.

Facilitation is a key aspect of professional health practice and indeed coaching. Facilitation is defined by Burrows (1997 p. 401) as "a goal orientated dynamic process in which participants work together in an atmosphere of genuine mutual respect, in order to learn through critical reflection". It is seen as person-centred and collaborative, a process of synthesis, of shared learning and a means of developing critical thinking. However, the actual role of the facilitator remains elusive and only vaguely specified (Haith-Cooper 2000). Rogers (1983, p. 189) maintained that a facilitator creates "an atmosphere of realness, of caring and of understanding listening". As a result, a coach as a facilitator has an active and supportive role in any setting to encourage the development of self-directed learning skills in ageing adults. Retirement coaches as facilitators can develop a style and skill base that promotes satisfaction and meets individual and group needs while balancing this to maintain the boundaries and clear outcomes.

Being facilitative and enabling will create a positive and collaborative relationship. The role of such a retirement coach in this context requires:

- The ability to create an affirmative climate for person-centred learning and development.
- The flexibility to cope with changing agendas.
- The opportunity to see the present and future as an opportunity and not as a challenge.
- The capability to respond to individual ageing adults' needs within a group/communal situation.
- The capacity to engage the ageing adult in reflective dialogue and critical thinking.

The style or approach presented by a coach as a facilitator can reflect one's own philosophical stance and unique personality, thus there will always be elements of difference (Clouston and Whitcombe 2005). It appears that these differences will either enhance or detract from the ageing adults' experiences depending on the needs of their respective peer group, the ability of the facilitator to meet them, and the congruence between learning style and perception. Professionals as retirement coaches will need to ensure that facilitation takes place to enable the ageing adult and not control them. This change in role will not be seen as an easy task but is fundamental to becoming an effective coach and facilitator (Rogers 1983, p. 189).

Johnson and Tinning (2001) argue that, by adopting a reflective approach, facilitators are offered an opportunity to explore their own actions and develop a level of self-awareness and responsiveness to others that can enable proactive change. Similarly, peer review systems and support from other colleagues can be seen as a means of enhancing the understanding of how a coach actually facilitates (Johnson and Tinning 2001). The group process itself will also enable facilitation by offering an opportunity for direct feedback from ageing adults and consequently give them an opportunity to be heard. This will not only offer a more equitable partnership but can enhance and build self-worth when the ageing adult's voice is valued. Enhancing such affirmative feelings, values and beliefs is encouraged through the retirement coach adopting an appreciative, alert and observing approach. As stated, using appreciative inquiry skills can assist both the coach and ageing adult to focus on opportunities rather than challenges. The professional as a retirement coach adopting an appreciative approach can help ageing adults:

- To let go of challenges – memories, experiences, routines and people.
- Embrace opportunities – hopes, dreams and aspirations and new friends.
- Celebrate life more as a gift and opportunity and live it to the moment.
- Express gratitude and appreciation as key life-giving enhancing emotions.
- To see the world through a happy, compassionate and renewed generosity of spirit.
- In response, retirement coaching can help ageing adults to build a more satisfying and fulfilling life by asking:
- What do you long for? – is it the perennial pursuit of happiness that continues into old age and contributes to the quality of your life?
- How will you enjoy daily life with less stress, anxiety, worry, and anger?

Retirement coaching therefore can help answer a key question of the ageing adult,

'What's next?' Questions such as:

- What are the issues and the opportunities in your current life?
- How will setting clear goals bring meaningful change to your life?
- When you reach your goal, how will you know? What will success look and feel like?
- Any external resources you will need to help achieve goals?
- If others are involved, what competency or skills do they need to help you?

Retirement coaching as a way to establish social worth

For ageing adults entering retirement, reactions to communal and societal attitudes can easily influence all aspects of the individual including their psychological, emotional and spiritual well-being. Potential feelings of being undervalued or disregarded by society are at times experienced by ageing adults, particularly when negative stereotypes or ageist generalisations are experienced. Such perceptions may also exacerbate feelings of under appreciation by society, contributing to negative feelings about the self and retirement. What may be more concerning, negative stereotypical views have often been reflected in government policies and in particular when reported by the media. What is often denied is the very fact that most ageing adults have and continue to contribute substantially to all aspects of society and therefore are deserving of greater appreciation and acknowledgment in employment, health and social care directives and policies. The need to develop resilience and self-determination is central to maintaining and promoting well-being and pride amongst ageing adults. In this context, autonomy and independence can be essential factors when building self-determination and self-worth.

Case study

Janice's confidence has been knocked lately. She took redundancy at 58 years old and has decided not to pursue further full-time paid employment. Most of her friends, however, have continued to work. This has left Janice feeling lonely. Her morale has been knocked and her self-esteem is low.

She has shared that she does not feel valued because when it comes to anything to do with pensions or finance in her position, some friends hold a negative judgmental perspective. She feels her expertise, professional skills, personal qualities and experiences are being undervalued.

Pause point

A mutual friend has put Janice in touch with you and encouraged her to seek your professional guidance with her emerging issues relating to her retirement.

Using an appreciative approach how would you begin to work/ coach with Janice?

How would you approach this in a way that was most affirming?

What more affirmative strategy can you personally adopt as a way to develop a more positive and self-determined change strategy?

Having put an initial strategy together on how you may best support Janice, next, consider your role with Janice once you have explored the following 3 Eye Model developed by Roberts and Machon (2015).

The '3 Eye Model' – an innovative framework for retirement coaching

The 3 Eye Model is one approach that can be applied to ascertain how ageing adults can positively change and develop during the transitional retirement period. Historically some view that life change is largely problematic and best described by a deficit-based theory (Kotter 1998). However, there appears to be an emerging trend to see such change as an opportunity rather than as a threat, a way forward rather than a step backwards. A more affirmative and appreciative view of change has the potential to create a path for positive psychology and the work of Seligman and Csikszentmihalyi (2000) who paved the way to understand the scientific study of positive human functioning and flourishing. Seligman (2002) explored what contributes to a fulfilling life well lived and showed how one's signature strengths relate to authentic happiness and abundant gratification. In support of this, Roberts and Machon (2010) developed an approach where the concept of the 3 Eye Model was created as a way to focus through a lens, to accommodate the '3 Eyes', of the coach, namely the:

- Analytical eye – more of a problem-focussed, often reactive lens
- Appreciative eye – more of an affirmative and reflective lens
- Creative eye – combined lens that can accommodate and includes the best of both – an expanded vision and band width of perception that can enable responsiveness and meaningful choice making

The model has the capacity to be:

- both simple and illustrative in its content and application
- integrative rather than partial or reductive
- offering insight to the opportunities as well as the challenges that professional health workers (and coaches) may face
- helping envision the clear developmental opportunities that can be chosen towards sustaining a best supportive and coaching practice

Pause point

When critically reflecting on your own professional performance as part of your continuing professional development:

What is your most vital resource as an individual and a professional developing coaching skills?

What qualities would you be wanting to enhance as a retirement coach?

How would you ensure that you get the best out of the ageing adult going through transitional retirement?

Make notes on your learning needs and what may be your professional development strategy?

The 3 Eyes of the professional and/or retirement coach

Here, the 3 Eyes will be explored further (adapted from Roberts and Machon 2015, pp. 53–58).

1. The Analytical eye – a problem-focussed lens

When one defaults into auto-pilot, one can adopt a particular way of seeing and vision – that of the analytical eye. This eye focuses upon the negative/challenging aspect rather than on the positive/opportunistic. Focussing excessively on the analytical eye – deficit-based thinking – will limit the coaching practice and effective support offered to the ageing adult. When considering some of the key limitations of working with this eye in practice, Roberts and Machon (2015) acknowledged the potential limitation of a professional as a coach to become:

- **Self-serving orientation** – being less concerned with the needs of the ageing adult and more in protecting and preserving one's self. The compulsion of the unconscious analytical eye is to affirm the sense of rightness by getting to the problem and the right answer. At times is it argued that the pressures of work in health and social care or otherwise often compel individuals to do so.

- **Political** – here there may be minimal capacity to accommodate the needs of the ageing adult. The viewpoint may be singular and judged to be absolutely right. This eye can show a tendency to be comfortable to debate but holding true to its absolute position of what it thinks is correct and right. The belief here is that there may be only one way of doing things and that is 'my way'. The analytical eye may be seen as a political eye.

- **Negative bias and cynicism** – here there is an automatic preoccupation with the 'not working' and negative; its view will focus on being problem-centred. Perceived negative bias can be unconscious and often even professionals can become unaware of its extent or influence on thinking and practice. Retirement coaches will feel compelled to get to the problem and then to rapidly evaluate with the intent to fix, to solve, to make it better. If one only looks for problems, the likelihood is that one will only find problems. This will create a cynical and negative edge to one's perspective on life. The coach in this context will automatically react rather than respond to the needs of the ageing adult. In reflection, one might consider what role the analytical eye may play in creating an insidious negative culture.

- **Cold detached and objectifying** – as an external observer, a retirement coach can come across as distant and detached, only looking in to assess rationally and objectively. It is by nature a differentiating eye, quick to judge this to be right and that to be wrong. It finds the problem and in so doing isolates this part from the whole. What this looks like in practice is that coaches will see the ageing adult more in part than as a whole person. This cold, detached objectification is what is often seen through the analytical eye and will be partial sightedness and blindness to the whole person.

- **Content focussed** – when being overtly content-focussed, the analytical eye has a tendency to be rational and preoccupied with facts and data – it is more quantitative in nature rather than qualitative. It can rapidly focus down in the content and detail and measures success more often by targets and form filling. In getting to the detail this eye misses the larger context and the opportunity to actively engage. It can be less interested to question and more to give the answer.

- **A non-empathic approach** – if the retirement coach takes the position of standing outside and looking in objectively, the analytical eye can devalue the importance of subjective experience *per se*. They may not be able to stand in the shoes of the ageing adult and offer an empathic response. Little value is placed on what someone is thinking, feeling or sensing and again may be more compelled to get to the facts and content of the interaction. This eye can have a limited resourcefulness and may quickly become depleted and exhausted.

- **Non–reflective practice** – a non-empathic eye is often unable to self-reflect. Everything can be judged to be either good or bad with a resulting set of action steps. The desire is to constantly evaluate, overlooking the value of the thoughts and feelings of the ageing adult. This non-reflective eye will lack the capacity to pace and pause and to question and engage – to be truly relational.

- **Reacting to the past** – missing present reality. Rather than responding to the present, a retirement coach's reaction will immediately go to memory and the past. This eye will overlook the need to reality check. It has a form of blindness, an inability to assess what is actually happening here and now. What they are not able to see is how they will be caught in reaction to and controlled by their thoughts and feelings rather than being able to reflect and respond to them.

- **Critical and judgemental** – One dimensional vision. Reactively, retirement coaches can be compelled to evaluate and critically appraise the situation. The compulsion to analyse and evaluate will be turned inward as well as outward. At times the coach can become the problem and judge themselves harshly. It will not be uncommon through this eye to be plagued with self-doubt and criticism. The un-awakened analytical eye appears to account for some neurotic tendencies. The result is that retirement coaches and the ageing adult alike will become critical and judgemental of themselves.

Being aware of each of these limitations can be a reminder to the professional as a retirement coach of the opportunity to expand their vision to consciously shift to a more appreciative and creative eye. Making such shifts consciously can profoundly impact the vision of the coach and indeed the ageing adult.

The following theme looks at the influence of the appreciative eye when working together with or in place of the analytical eye.

2. The Appreciative eye – more of an affirmative eye

Retirement coaches can learn to focus through the appreciative eye in practice especially when caught in the un-awakened analytical eye.

- **An integrative eye** – When an appreciative eye is opened, one will be encouraged to seek insight, essentially the capacity to witness, reflect upon, accommodate and respond to subjective experiences. Whereas the analytical eye takes an objective external view, the appreciative eye can be both internal and subjective. This experiential eye will be able to reflect on one's own and the ageing adults' inner-subjective experience and is more interested to consider and include the value of feelings, thoughts and senses. This innate capacity to include subjective experience will mean that coaching through this lens can be more flexible, accommodating a fuller and more authentic picture of oneself and others. This has the potential to be a powerfully integrative eye with a wider bandwidth than the analytical eye. It will be able to significantly expand awareness, negating the tendency to automatically jump to conclusions based on the partial and limited data and perspective of the analytical eye. In opening the appreciative eye, one will become more open minded. Fredrickson (1998) argues that this open mindedness and broadening mindset offer both indirect and long term adaptive benefits.

- **Awareness of self and others – 2D (Dimensional) vision** – The appreciative eye has a 2D (Dimensional) vision, being able to accommodate the experiences of both the professional as a retirement coach and the ageing adult. Its ability to take several different perspectives and to reflect upon what the coach will be feeling, thinking and sensing can create the capacity to attune to the ageing adult's experience – especially emotional and non-verbal signals. In contrast to the analytical eye, the appreciative considers fostering the natural ability to build rapport and engagement – to be more relational.

- **An empathic stance** – The capacity to be aware of one's own subjective experience and that of others will highlight the innate empathic ability of the appreciative eye. This is the capacity to be able to 'stand in the shoes' of the ageing adult and to reflect with them about their experience. This will allow the professional or retirement coach to attune to, and be more aware of, the wishes and wants of the ageing adult. In being able to relate to another in this way, it will be possible to move beyond evaluation and quieten judgemental and critical activity. Through the appreciative lens the retirement coach will be able to build trust by fostering the ability to attend fully, to establish rapport, engagement and personal empowerment.

- **Positive bias** – In the absence of a compulsion to problem solve there will be space for one's interest and curiosity to motivate a more relational approach. Rather than trying to get to the answer, a coach will begin to more naturally seek to question the ageing adult. Interest, calmness, curiosity are all qualities that engender a more appreciative and positive approach to work and contrasts markedly with the negative bias of the analytical eye.

- **Questioning rather than answering** – No longer feeling compelled to answer, looking at retirement with an appreciative eye will motivate the coach to more effectively question the ageing adult in a more person- centred manner. This eye is no longer compelled to evaluate and as such, develops space to pause and the prospect of creative uncertainty. Learning how 'not to know' will foster the ability of the professional as a retirement coach to listen more intently and respond to ageing adults' wishes and needs.

- **Working in the present with presence (In the here and now)** – The appreciative eye can self-reflect and is able to be present and to see current reality simply as it is. This eye will assist the coach to make a clear assessment of the current situation. Being in the present will mean that ageing adults are more able to harness and focus their concentration intently. Equally, the more the coach is able to gift their attention to the ageing adult, the more their presence may be experienced.

- **Pace and pause** – The appreciative eye is able to bring more of pace to work and is comfortable to pause and reflect. This ability to be still and stop can at times prevent the retirement coach from making premature judgements, since they are no longer compelled to evaluate and rapidly conclude. The coach will be less distracted and able to concentrate effectively on the actual coaching role.

- **Accommodating vulnerability** – The ability of the appreciative eye to reflect upon subjective experience means that professionals as retirement coaches will begin to accommodate both vulnerability as well as the strengths of the ageing adult and themselves. The analytical eye in rejecting subjective experience can at times create the mask of the perfectionist. It is unable to consider vulnerability and limitation, make believing that in our professional role we are perfectly right and fine. The appreciative eye, in contrast, is able to reflect upon limitation and consider needs in relation to vulnerability and strengths. Through this eye, the ageing adults' fears, doubts and anxieties about retirement can find expression. The appreciative eye can therefore tune into their needs and more fully enable resourcefulness of the ageing adult and, indeed, oneself as a coach.

In reflection, the appreciative eye offers a more open, conditional and mindful approach and Langer (1989, 1997, 2000, 2005b) has illustrated how such coaching intervention can result in more engaged effective learning, greater competence and creativity, more positive feelings, less burn out, better health and even increased charisma, including in retirement.

3. The Creative Eye – the effective bringing together of the analytical and appreciative lens

The limitations of the analytical eye are negated by the strengths of the appreciative eye. Imagine placing the analytical and appreciative eye together, as if they were, in essence, two faces of the same coin; the limitations of one will be cancelled by the strengths of the other (see Table 1), adapted from Machon (2010, p.47). In combination, a third eye is formed that offers the strengths of both (Table 2) and something more still – a truly unlimited and responsive way of seeing.

Table 1
How limitations and strengths of the analytical and appreciative eyes are complimentary

Analytical	Appreciative
Unable to expand awareness	Expands awareness
Grounds/contracts	Unable to ground/contract
Non-reflective	Reflective
Reactive	Able to pace and pause
Non-empathic	Empathic
Evaluate and action plan	Unable to evaluate and action plan

Table 2
The collective strengths of the awakened analytical and appreciative eye

Self-serving	In service of other
Objective	Subjective
Contracts awareness	Expands awareness
Reactive	Reflective
Differentiating	Integrating
Isolates the part	Integrates different parts
Non-empathic	Empathic
Answering	Questioning

Pause point

Recall the time in your professional life when you were practicing at your very best.

What were the characteristics of this experience?

What did you experience? How were you being?

What were you doing?

The creative eye informs and defines our best practice as professionals and enables the following fundamentally key characteristics of an effective retirement coach:

Unconditional positive regard

Together in the combination of the analytical and appreciative eyes, the creative eye of the retirement coach sees with unconditional positive regard. This describes the offering of support and acceptance without judgment or condition, allowing the ageing adult to accept oneself and not be caught in others' judgment of their value and worth.

It is a capacity to be fully present to the other, to attune and empathise whilst having the ability to also step back. This ability to keep this respectful detachment whilst demonstrating care requires the retirement coach to be present, empathic and equally responsive and facilitative.

Awareness of the present, past and future

In the synthesis of the appreciative and analytical eyes the bandwidth of awareness through the creative eye will greatly expand and contract. As such, this is an uncompromised eye. It can concentrate fully and assess current reality and what the present moment requires. It is equally comfortable to connect with and recall past history as required and to enable the setting of a desired future goal.

An unlimited eye – uncompromised and responsive

The creative eye can be responsive, an uncompromised and highly flexible eye – it can question and/or help the ageing adult to answer; it can focus on context and/or content; it can expand awareness by inviting the ageing adult to consider options and it can contract awareness, helping them to plan by identifying the choices and next steps they wish to take. This eye can view each situation from many different perspectives (appreciative aspect) and, in combination with the awakened analytical eye, is able to evaluate and action plan at will.

How the appreciative eye can limit:

- The lens of the appreciative eye is unable to ground, contract and focus.
- The appreciative eye can lack structure and is unable to ground; both are considered key to action planning.
- This eye may be unable to effectively assess, evaluate, prioritise or plan.
- It can easily generate options but then has no capacity to focus down.

Pause point

Consider at this stage how these limitations may in fact be the complementary strengths of the analytical eye.

The 3 D (Dimensional) varifocal lens

The lens of the creative eye has a more unlimited capacity. Imagine it to be like a varifocal lens. The lens of the creative eye will be totally flexible and can adapt and compensate to each and all of the limitations of one's sight. This reminds us once more of the flexibility of this lens and how it can accommodate many different perspectives, fostering equally and at will: a mental, emotional, physical and spiritual awareness and response. In addition, the creative eye will also be able to step out and look beyond the individual and relational (the 2D vision of the appreciative eye element) to consider how the wider collective (the 3D aspect) will impact and influence.

The motivational eye

The creative eye can be motivational in that it is able to engage the will of the ageing adult, their ability to identify choice and take action. What motivates change is when we link choice with our values, beliefs and purpose. The creative eye can facilitate this process, thus enabling the ageing adult to express personal values, belief and sense of purpose. This remembering is equally important for the practitioner, recognising their values, empowering belief and recalling one's purpose – why one chooses to do what one does – sets one's vital compass bearings and brings motivation to work. This awareness affirms and enforces one's commitment to care, brings meaning to work and ensures resourcefulness in practice. Through the creative eye one can truly begin to work with the needs of the ageing adult. Baumeister (1991 p. 301) notes four dimensions, a need for:

1. Purpose – believing in something to move towards and desire
2. Values – things one values, that make one feel good and positive and help decide what is right or wrong. Goals shaped by values create actions and decisions that have great meaning.
3. Self-efficacy – that one is able to control and manage attention and make a difference
4. Self-worth – that one is essentially good and worthwhile

Ultimately when these different aspects of need are combined, when both the ageing adult and/or retirement coach are clear of their purpose, values and they are experiencing personal efficacy and worth, then life and occupations are experienced as meaningful.

Making meaning

It is important to consider the role of the retirement coach in helping or enabling the ageing adult to make meaning of their retirement situation, as a key step towards engaging their resourcefulness and progress towards well-being. Recall the analytical eye, its reactivity and lack of choice. Seligman and Maier (1967) notes how meaningless suffering is the cause of endless human misery, how this steals away the sense of control and blinds the sense of purpose – as a result, one can develop a learned helplessness. Making meaning is central to both retirement coach and ageing adult and holds the potential for the opportunity of growth. Csikszentmihalhyi (1992) expresses that the meaning of life is making meaning – whatever it is and wherever it comes from. Gazzaninga (1985 and 1993) explains how the left hemisphere of the human brain interprets and gives meaning to situations by making connections between aspects, even when there is no actual connection. When the retirement coach enables the ageing adult to make their connections and meaning of their situation and to discover what choices they have, it can make a profound difference to how the ageing adult approaches all aspects of retirement and their sense of control, engagement and motivation. Realising one's choice will bridge the depressive feeling of no choice with a positive intent and motivation to engage one's will to change. Having choices can always be interpreted meaningfully. Note how realising choices can transform the ageing adult from feeling a victim to be more empowered and actively engaged in the transitional retirement process.

Accommodating a spiritual context

The opening of a creative eye offers the retirement coach and ageing adult a further dimension of awareness, recognising one's part within the whole, discovering hope and affirming one's faith in 'something more'. This spiritual context can inform a personal belief system, irrespective of the specificity of a chosen belief and faith. The belief in something 'larger than' and realising our connection, one's part and place within this, can give an important context to life and occupations. This can potentially bring great relevance and meaning to challenging situations. An awareness of such personal beliefs will positively sustain the retirement coach in their professional practice in times of crisis. For the ageing adult, recalling empowering beliefs and a sense of purpose will positively build one's sense of resourcefulness and empowerment.

Eliciting resilience and resourcefulness

The creative eye is a resilient eye in that it can discover opportunity in adversity. Its ability to look at things from many different perspectives offers the chance to reframe challenging scenarios to offer opportunity for the ageing adult. Imagine asking the following question: 'What are you being invited to learn through this period of transition?' This is not about making the situation easier, but more reframing the situation and working with compassion to invite the ageing adult to discover their choice and resourcefulness as an essential potential step towards health and well-being. This experience will significantly build resourcefulness and give confidence to find choice and respond positively to adversity in retirement.

Working with compassion

The creative eye will allow several unique qualities and capabilities to emerge into a caring and coaching role that include and yet also extend beyond the potential of the analytical and appreciative alone. One such quality is compassion. When the professional and retirement coach demonstrates empathy, one will be able to 'step into the shoes' of the ageing adult and attune to their unique situation. In offering unconditional positive regard, the gift of one's full attention with intimacy and to model a detachment with warmth and care – one will be able to build upon an empathic response to consider the question, 'how can one help or how can the ageing adult help to relieve potential anxiety in relation to their situation and future?' Professionals and retirement coaches can demonstrate compassionate intervention in practice when they both empathise and enable action to help relieve challenges.

Working with dignity

With the opening of the appreciative eye, professionals and retirement coaches will develop a more non-judgemental position with others. When seeing through the lens of the creative eye, one can take a further step in offering unconditional positive regard and move from being non-condemning to be more wholly accepting of the individual. In experiencing unconditional positive regard, the ageing adult will feel safe and trusting and is able to explore their own mind, to understand their emotions and potentially feel soothed. The ageing adult will feel met, understood and held and therefore, comfortable to share experiences and disclose. The creative eye invites the ageing adult to be authentic and to work with integrity to include their vulnerabilities as well as their strengths with the intention of their full engagement in their transitional retirement. In this, the ageing adults' humanity will be acknowledged. Practising with dignity involves remembering and respecting the innate value of the ageing adult as a human being. This approach supports the belief of the creative eye that the individual innately has all the personal resources necessary for their growth, well-being and fulfilment. The role of the retirement coach is to see potential and invite resourcefulness in the ageing adult and to encourage self-care and positive creativity of thinking and doing.

Pause point

Recall the times when you have demonstrated coaching skills at your very best.

What is characteristic of this experience?

What do you notice about your attention? Where is your attention?

Record this from a place of personal and professional reflection.

Remember Janice? Have a look at her situation below again. Ask yourself the same pause point questions, and has anything changed with the additional insights of the 3 Eye Model?

Janice's confidence has been knocked lately. She took redundancy at the age of 58 years old and has decided not to pursue further full-time paid employment. Most of her social friends, however, have continued to work. This has left Janice feeling lonely. Her morale has been knocked and her self-esteem is at an all-time low.

She has shared that she does not feel valued because when it comes to anything to do with pensions or finance in her position, society holds a negative judgmental perspective. She feels her expertise, professional, personal qualities and experiences are being undervalued.

Pause point

Using the 3 Eye Model how would you now work/coach with Janice?

What more appreciative and affirmative strategy would you now adopt as a way to enable and develop a more balanced, positive and self-determined change strategy for Janice?

With the 3 Eye Model in mind and considering its application as a coach, the transition to retirement is seen as a mixture of the expected and unexpected. Ageing adults who decide to retire do not do so at a whim, the process is often very well thought through and informed. Professionals and the retirement coach, in private, leisure, health and social care environments, can aspire to best support and enable individuals and groups through this important transition. Being able to maximise on one's own personal and professional skill set is key. Also, being able to work with a variety of evidenced frameworks, models and theories including, as illustrated, the application of the 3 Eye Model. Such frameworks offer a structure and a platform to empower ageing adults to diversify efforts to exciting recreational activities, hobbies, family support, voluntary and non-voluntary work, memberships of clubs and organisations that will offer positive opportunities for constructing a life with occupations and friendships beyond the work place. Making a successful and positive transition using the 3 Eye Model will bring about major life-affirming readjustments in the absence of traditional work, maybe less social contact and a potentially decreasing income, in the building of sustainable and comfortable occupations of choice. Ageing adults often carry a wealth of nostalgic memories and experiences with them into retirement, and such thoughts can inform the need for a life to be well lived in the here and now. Being supported and exploring how to be more fully engaged in purposeful and meaningful occupations is crucial. Ageing adults will need to acknowledge that their own mortality can be used as a reminder and a motivation to complete exciting activities, projects, promises, aspirations and tasks that may have laid dormant. Ageing adults do not have to do it all alone; here the presence of the retirement coach can truly be vital.

CHAPTER 8

FINAL THOUGHTS

All too often societies seem to concentrate on perceiving retirement as a problem. The focus at times is on what is not working, what an ageing adult fails to, or cannot do and the overall perception by some that old age and retirees are a burden. This is not true of all societies where ageing is celebrated and more respected. It is important to reinforce the very individual nature of ageing and its relationship to transitional retirement and beyond. It is important to stress the belief that each individual's life experience, spirituality, values, beliefs, culture, sexuality, family, career and so on will result in a unique retirement transition experience. There cannot be a universal approach to the subject area. This said, reframing a negative perception to positively focus on what does work by valuing and recognising the significant and positive contribution that ageing adults as retirees make to all aspects of society is key. Appreciative inquiry proposes and advocates such perceptions and their application in, and to life is key to transitional success. This means making the most of what works; amplifying it; understanding the conditions that support what works; and concentrating on improving those conditions. For the retirement coach, it changes the question from what the problem is, what does not work in this transitional period and how it can be fixed, to what does work and how can one do more of it. This can guide one to view retirement much more positively and appreciatively – as something to look forward to.

The primary aim of introducing appreciative inquiry and the 3 Eye Model to retirement coaching is important for a variety of reasons and for a wide spectrum of different people. It has the potential to empower all to influence what appears at times to be an over emphasis on seeing old age and retirement negatively, a barrier, a burden and a challenge. Instead, seeing the world with an appreciative eye has the capacity to see ageing and retirement as an opportunity, by seeing potential, aiming for the very best, creating and sustaining the energy needed to act into a more positively envisioned future. From the moment one is born, we age, so we are all ageing, we age as each day passes and therefore at what point do we become an ageing adult?

So, what would it be like if one were to let it be, and allow the individual to make that very personal decision and to celebrate that landmark and rite of passage? What is clear, working in partnership with ageing adults is an exciting consideration and one that can positively impact on how individuals make the transition into retirement in a much more affirmative manner. Its potential will create a new foundation for enabling positive, transformative change in how individuals perceive their own understanding of ageing and their retirement transition, and how professional facilitation in coaching can empower and enable those ageing adults to manage change.

Pepin and Deutscher (2011) have called for more research evidence into the outcome of working with ageing adults in transitional retirement, and they conclude that in future, professionals (retirement coaches) must take more time to listen to ageing adults' lived experiences in order to learn. This will, in return, enable such ageing adults to identify areas of interest as a way to engage in activities that are truly meaningful to foster a positive occupational adaptation to retirement. Hewitt et al. (2010) have expressed concern that a lot of research to date has generally focussed primarily on the preparation for retirement. This suggests that more research is required into how ageing adults manage and potentially thrive whilst in retirement. Increased evidenced and knowledge on how ageing adults in transition achieve meaningful occupational balance can inevitably assist retirement coaches to empower individuals and enable them to make the transition effectively in a more affirmative person-centred way.

Appreciative inquiry is one effective approach to such research and it provides a platform for the health and social care professional as a retirement coach to utilise the 3 Eye Model as a practice framework to focus on the whole person and, in particular, on the more positive and affirmative aspects of retirement and occupational engagement. This highlights the potential to apply appreciative inquiry into coaching practice (Roberts, 2011). Rubin, Kerrell and Roberts (2011) carried out a qualitative study on appreciative inquiry as a learning tool in the education of occupational therapists (potential future retirement coaches) and found that the approach 'changes the focus from the practitioner to the client' (p. 236). Rubin et al. also states 'clients benefited from the focus on their own wishes rather than what the therapist believed would be advantageous' (p. 236). This demonstrates that implementing appreciative inquiry in both education and practice can potentially enhance client-centred practice and collaborative working (Rubin et al. 2011. p. 239), a central aspect of how coaches may approach working with ageing adults. Applying the principles of appreciative inquiry and the 3 Eye Model with ageing adults will simply mean that the retirement coach continues to look and focus primarily at the affirmative opportunities this important life stage can offer. Such a vision can be positive, exciting and life changing. A retirement coach working with appreciative inquiry and emerging models of practice such as the 3 Eye Model can encourage a more positive self-perspective in the context of transitional retirement and beyond. Importantly, it will also guide health and social care professionals as potential retirement coaches to challenge any negative or preconceived mindsets or beliefs about this life stage and events. The idea of using the lens of the appreciative eye assumes that in every aspect of life something works (Roberts and Machon 2015), and as such appreciative inquiry and the 3 Eye Model will open up the context in which some negative and problematic perspectives can be changed or balanced. This will offer the opportunity for the retirement coach to introduce the probability of a much more affirmative, appreciative and creative outlook on ageing adults and their lives in retirement. This paradoxical approach mirrors our deepest understanding of human nature since it views ageing adults as individuals with some challenges and problems, who are in a continual process of becoming more whole and complete. This approach considers both what is and also what will be. A negative preconceived idea about ageing adults will devalue some peoples' understanding of human nature by judging ageing adults in transitional retirement as a problem needing to be solved. This is often overly portrayed in some media stereotypes of growing old. If professionals, for example, see an ageing adult only as a problem (what they cannot do) they become blind to their full human potential (what they can do) and what they may become and what great contribution they continue to make in all aspects of society. The intention is to apply this notion to transitional retirement. Since the appreciative statements are grounded in real experiences and history, ageing adults will know how to repeat their success. The idea, therefore, in planning and engaging in transitional retirement is to approach prospective challenges with an appreciative eye.

In including mindfulness as a potential and practical retirement coaching intervention, it clearly advocates the belief that virtually everyone may benefit from being more mindful in their personal and occupational lives. Many believe that the evidenced benefits of mindfulness include enhanced flexibility, improved concentration, more self-control, emotional intelligence, objectivity in the world and better mental clarity. Such benefits add to the human potential for kindness, compassion, dignity and acceptance. Langer (1989, 1997, 2000 and 2005b) believes that mindfulness can encourage individuals to actively keep their mind open and more objective. This is a more open and conditional approach that potentially results in more engagement, effective learning, greater competence, more positive feelings, greater creativity, less occupational burn-out, better health and even increased charisma (Machon 2010). When effectively studied and applied, mindfulness can be beneficial in areas such as reducing levels of stress, increasing levels of emotional intelligence, raising levels of self-awareness and awareness of others. It will also increase interpersonal sensitivity and communication skills between an ageing adult and the retirement coach. Most importantly, it assists in lowering levels of psychological distress by raising levels of well-being and life satisfaction as individuals manage change. Having the insight and skill to inwardly reflect as a way to consider the value of subjective experience means that a more mindful approach to retirement coaching is achieved essentially for both coach and client. Responding in this manner, rather than reacting to subjective experience, is seen as key to the coach's ability to focus, attend, self-manage and be in the moment with the ageing adult – to be present. Mindful practice in this way provides a platform for the retirement coach to be much more in service of the ageing adult and, in turn, of themselves. Such a relationship is central to developing affirmative, enabling, empowering and responsive retirement coaching.

Dealing successfully with demographic change means shedding outdated stereotypes and changing mindsets about retirement and the process of ageing – we are all ageing and growing old! Debates about demographic change too often focuses on financial issues, extra costs on the state, health/social care, and changes in the 'dependency ratio'. It is true that these future costs pose real challenges to our welfare state and raise questions about the extent to which it is right for one generation to commit our successors. Without doubt these challenges must be addressed by modern day society. However, they must not dominate thinking about ageing. Longer occupational lives can be something to celebrate, as long as there is a healthy work – life balance, seizing the positive opportunities they present will make sustainable solutions possible. For governments, the challenge is to change attitudes and preconceptions about what an ageing society means and to stimulate innovative ideas and technologies to transform ageing lives. It is important to seize the opportunity to rethink policies and approaches to public services, in order to foster true independence and choice in mid-life and for ageing citizens as a way to help them improve their own quality of life. For that to happen, one must explode the myth that mid-life and ageing is a barrier to a positive contribution to the economy and society, through work and through active occupational engagement in the community. It is argued that longer life is a blessing where the extra years are fulfilling and active. They should not be years of inaction and exclusion. A personal responsibility rests on each individual to plan and provide for a different life course that is also better. For business, a changing customer base offers new markets. But the workforce is seen as changing too, and this must prompt new thinking about job design, recruitment, retention, the role of creativity and employer responsibilities.

In services that are crucial to retaining independence, ageing adults are still often treated as passive recipients rather than active consumers with their own views about their needs. Chronological age should not be a barrier to choice, and control of one's own personal life to the maximum level possible, in particular when it comes to creativity and meaningful occupations. Whatever the results of published studies and the characteristics currently proposed for work, occupation and creativity, it needs to be acknowledged that the mid-life in the context of ageing is a relatively new area of research interest, with comparatively few research studies on which to base the claims of a universal mid-life transition. Such theoretical sources argue that a focus in this time period on productive output and social acclaim is inadequate to portray and understand the events occurring within work and the creative process. This time period in the adult life is under-explored compared with childhood and adolescence. Those sources suggest that attention to the characteristics of occupations and creativity in this time period, and that the phenomenology of creative work indicative of the experience of ageing, would yield new understandings of occupational engagement.

It appears that society in general is beginning to appreciate that ageing adults can be key players in economic, political and organisational success, in paid and voluntary services and as such, employers have a huge role to play in enabling society to adjust effectively to a new balance of life. This is now being supported by equality legislation. With that in mind, ageism must be discarded. To dispel ageism, individuals in the mid- life and beyond must be seen as being of value to modern day society; but what is this value? Health and social care professionals as coaches may want ageing adults to succeed into their retirement, and they can empower and enable them to achieve success using whatever approach seems most effective. If it's the 3 Eye Model, all the better as far as this book is concerned. Beyond success, flourishing is important to ageing adults and to retirement coaching. If coaches find ways of enabling ageing adults in retirement to flourish, they will have done their jobs well. If they can help ageing adults accept themselves as fully capable, creative and autonomous agents in making choices, if they can help them master their environments, have positive relations with those around them, and pursue a purpose about which they feel passionate, then they have contributed to a more empowered and effective group of people in society.

In Thomas Moore's Soulful Ageing work (2017), he speaks of retirement as … "marking the end of a particular form of work, but all along other kinds have also been addressing the longings of the soul. By doing service, volunteering, working at a hobby, gardening, taking care of the house, studying, and even travelling. These may all be forms of work that speak to our deep hopes and wishes. Obviously, they can continue after formal retirement, so that in this simple way we continue to work, and your soul benefits. Some people enjoy retirement, being released from a job that has occupied them for many years. For others, retirement doesn't make any sense. They will continue to do their job as long as they are able. The work we do in retirement could be more important than ever.

REFERENCES

Agahi, N. & Parker, M.G. (2005) Are today's older people more active than their predecessors? Participation in leisure-time activities in Sweden in 1992 and 2002. Ageing & Society, 25 pp. 925–941

Age Concern (2005). Making more of Life. http://www.ageconcern.org.uk/AgeConcern/News_967.htm (Accessed 18/05/16).

Bachkirova,T. (2011). Developmental Coaching – working with the self. Open University Press. McGraw- Hill Education. London.

Ball, V., Corr, S., Knight, J. & Lowis, M.J. (2007) An Investigation into the Leisure Occupations of Older Adults. British Journal of Occupational Therapy, 70(9) pp. 393–400.

Barnes, H. & Parry, J. (2004) Renegotiating identity and relationships: man and women's adjustments to retirement. Ageing & Society, 24 pp. 213–233.

Bash, A (2004). Issues in clinical nursing: Spirituality. Journal of Clinical Nursing 13,11–16.

Baumeister, R., F. (1991). Meanings of life. Guilford Press.

Bowling, A. (2008) Enhancing later life: How older people perceive active ageing. Ageing & Mental Health, 12(3) pp. 293–301.

Boyd, N.M. & D.S. Bright (2007). "Appreciative Inquiry As A Mode Of Action Research For A Community Psychology." Journal of Community Psychology, Vol.35, no. 8.

Bozio, A, Crawford, R & Tetlow, G (2010) The History of the State Pensions in the UK: 1948–2010. London: Institute of Fiscal Studies.

Brougham, R.R. & Walsh D.A. (2009) Early and late retirement exits. International Journal of Aging & Human Development, 69(4) pp. 267–286

Burholt,V. & Dobbs,C. (2013). 'Research on rural ageing: where have we got to and where are we going in Europe?' Journal of Rural Studies. Vol 28, pp 432–46.

Burrows, D. E. (1997) Facilitation: A Concept analysis, Journal of Advanced Nursing, 25, 396–404.

Cebulla, A., Butt, S. & Lyon, N. (2007) Working beyond the state pension age in the United Kingdom: the role of working time flexibility and the effects on the home. Ageing & Society, 27 pp. 849–867.

Claxton, G. (2004). Proximal spirituality; why the brains of angels are different from ours, in D.Lorimer (ed) Science, Consciousness & Ultimate Reality. Exeter:Imprint Academic , pp 129–44.

Clouston, T.J. & Whitcombe, S,W. (2005), An emerging person centred model for problem-based learning. Journal of Further and Higher Education. Vol 29, No 3, June 2005. pp 265–275.

Cooperrider, D. L. & D.Whitney (2000). A Positive Revolution in Change: Appreciative Inquiry, in D.Cooperrider, P.F.Sorensen, D. Whitney and T.F. Yaeger eds., Appreciative Inquiry: Rethinking Human Organization Toward a Positive Theory of Change, Stripes Publishing, Champaign, Illinois Cooperrider, D. & Whitney. D. (2005). Appreciative Inquiry: A Positive Revolution in Change. Berret-Koehler Publishing.

Cooperrider,D. & Strivastva, R. (1987). Appreciative Inquiry in Organizational Life. In Woodman, T. & Pasmore.M. (eds). Research on Organizational Change and Development, Vol, 1. JA1 Press.

Csikszentmihalyi, M. (1996). Creativity: flow and the psychology of discovery and innovation. Harper-Collins Publishers. New York.

Csikszentmihalyi, M. (1992). Flow: The psychology of happiness. London: Rider and Company. p 217.

Dane, E. (2011). Paying attention to mindfulness and its effects on task performance in the workplace. Journal of Management. 37 (4), pp 997–1018.

Davey, A. & Szinovacz, M.E. (2004) Dimensions of Marital Quality and Retirement. Journal of Family Issues, 25(4) pp. 431–464.

Dew, J. & Yorgason, J. (2010). Economic pressure and the marital conflict in retirement-aged couples. Journal of Family Issues, 31(2) pp. 164–188.

Directgov (2010). Pensions and Retirement Planning. http://www.direct.gov.uk/en/Pensionsandretirementplanning/index.htm [accessed 04/10/2010].

Estes, C. L., Biggs, S. & Phillipson, C. (2003) Social Theory, Social Policy and Ageing: a critical introduction. Maidenhead: Open University Press.

Everard, K.M. (1999) The Relationship Between Reasons for Activity and Older Adult Well-Being. Journal of Applied Gerontology, 18(3) pp. 325–340.

Fairhurst, E. (2003) New Identities in Ageing: Perspectives on Age, Gender and Life After Work. In: Arber, S., Davidson, K. & Ginn, J. (eds) Gender and Ageing: Changing Roles and Relationships, pp. 31–46.

Fitzgerald, S. P, Murrell, K.L. & H.L. Newman (2001). Appreciative inquiry – the new frontier, in J. Waclawski and A.H. Church (Eds.), Organization development: Data driven methods for change. San Francisco: Jossey-Bass Publishers, pp 203–221.

Francis, R (2013). Report of the Mid Staffordshire NHS FoundationTrust Public Inquiry: The Mid Staffordshire NHS Foundation Trust. Public Inquiry. London: The Stationery Office.

Fredrickson, B,L. (1998) What good are positive emotions? Review of general Psychology. 2. 300–319.

Gagliardi, C. Spazzafumo, L. Marcellini, F. Mollenkopf, H. Ruopilla, I. Tacken, M. & Szemann, Z. (2007) The outdoor mobility and leisure activities of older people in five European countries. Ageing & Society,. 27 pp. 683–700

Harper, S. (2006) Ageing Societies: myths, challenges and opportunities. London: Hodder Education.

Garland, E & Gaylord, S. (2009). Envisioning a future contemplative science of mindfulness: Fruitful methods and new content for the next wave of research. Complimentary Health Practice Review, 14 (1), 3–9.

Gazzaninga, M. S. (1985). The Social Brain. New York: Basic books.

Gazzaninga, M. S. (1993). Brain mechanisms and conscious experience. In Experimental and Theoretical Studies of Consciousness. Ciba Foundation Symposia series, no. 174. Chichester: Wiley. pp. 247–62.

Gilbert, P (2014). Mindful Compassion. New Harbinger Publishers Oakland. CA.

Gilleard, C. & Higgs, P. (2000) Cultures of Ageing: Self, citizen and the Body. Harlow: Prentice Hall.

Gran, B. (2008) Shifts in public-private provision of retirement income: a four-country comparison. Research on Ageing, 30(5) pp. 507–542

Haith-Cooper, M. (2000) Problem-based learning within health professional education. What is the role of the lecturer? Nurse Education Today, 20, p. 267–272.

Harper, S. (2006) Ageing Societies: myths, challenges and opportunities. London: Hodder Education.

Hewitt, A., Howie, L. & Feldman, S. (2010) Retirement: What will you do? A narrative inquiry of occupation-based planning for retirement:

Implications for practice. Australian Occupational Therapy Journal, 57(1) pp. 8–16

Jaques,E. (1965). Death and the Mid – Life Crisis. International Journal of Psychoanalysis. 1965, Vol 46, p. 502–514.

Jonsson, H., Borell, L., & Sadlo, G. (2000) Retirement: an occupational transition with consequences for temporality, balance and meaning of occupations. Journal of Occupational Science. 7 (1) 29–37.

Johnston-Taylor, E., (2007) What Do I Say? Talking with Patients about Spirituality, USA: Templeton Foundation Press.

Johnson, A, K. & Tinning ,R, S. (2001). Meeting the Challenge of Problem Based Learning : Developing the Facilitators, Nurse Education Today. 21, p 161–169.

Kabat-Zinn, J. (1994). Wherever You Go, There You Are: Mindfulness Meditation in Everyday Life, Hyperion, New York.

Katz, S. (2000) Busy Bodies: Activity, Aging, and the Management of Everyday Life. Journal of Ageing Studies, 14(2) pp. 135–152.

Kielhofner, G. (2008) Model of Human Occupation: theory and application. (4th ed). Baltimore: Lippincott Williams and Wilkins.

Kilewer, S.P. & Saultz, J., (2006) Healthcare and spirituality, UK: Radcliffe Publishing Ltd.

Kim, J. (2009) Early retirement in the three types of welfare states. Research on Aging. 31(5) pp. 520–548.

Kim, J.E. & Moen, P. (2001). Is retirement good or bad for subjective well-being? Current Direction in Psychological Science, 10(3) pp. 83–86.

Kotter (1998). Why transformation efforts. fail. Havard Business Review of Change. pp 1–20

Kulick, L. (2001). The impact of men's and women's retirement on marital relations: a comparative analysis. Journal of Women & Ageing 13(2) pp. 21–37

Kulick, L. (2002) Equality in marriage, marital satisfaction, and life satisfaction: A comparative analysis of pre-retired and retired men and women in Israel. Families in Society, 83(2) pp. 197–207.

Künemund, H. & Kolland, F. (2007) Work and Retirement. In: Bond, J., Peace, S., Dittman-Kohli, F. & Westerhof, G. (eds) Ageing in Society. London: Sage, pp. 167–185.

Langer, E. (1989). Mindfulness. New York. NY: Perseus books.

Langer, E. (1997). The Power of Mindful Learning. New York. NY: Perseus books.

Langer, E. (2000). Mindful Learning. Current Directions in Psychological Science, 9 (6), pp 220–223.

Langer, E. (2005a). On becoming an artist: Reinventing yourself through mindful creativity. New York, NY: Ballantine Books.

Langer, E. (2005b). Mindfulness versus Positive evaluation. In C.R. Snyder and S.J. Lopez, (eds). Handbook of Positive Psychology Oxford: OUP, pp. 214–30.

Legarth, K.H., Ryan, S. & Avlund, K. (2005). The most important activity and the reasons for that experience reported by a Danish population at age 5 years. British Journal of Occupational Therapy, 68(11), pp. 501–508.

LeMesurier, N. (2006). 'The contribution of older people in rural community and citizenship' in P.Lowe and L. Speakman (eds) The ageing countryside: the growing older population in rural England. London. Age Concern, pp 133–46.

Levinson, D. (1996). A Conception of Adult Development. American Psychologist. 1986. Vol 41 (1), pp 3–13.

Lewin, K. (1951). Field Theory in Social Science. Harper and Row, New York.

Lindauer, M. S, Orwoll, L. & Kelley, M.C (1997). Aging Artists on the Creativity of Their Old Age. Creativity Research Journal, Vol 10. Pt 2 and 3, p 133–152.Litwin, H. & Shiovitz-Ezra, S. (2006). The association between activity and well-being in later life: What really matters? Ageing & Society, 26(2) pp. 225–242.

Ludema, J.D, D. L. Cooperrider & F.J. Barrett (2001). Appreciative Inquiry: the Power of the Unconditional Positive Question, in Peter Reason and Hilary Bradbury Eds. The Handbook of Action Research, Sage. Ludema, J. D, D. L.Cooperrider & F. J. Barrett (2006). Appreciative Inquiry: the Power of the Unconditional Positive Question, in Peter Reason and Hilary Bradbury Eds., The Handbook of Action Research, Sage. Machon, A. (2010). The Coaching Secret. – how to be an exceptional coach. Harlow. Essex. Pearson education Ltd.

Maguire, P. (2001). Uneven Ground: Feminisms and Action Research, in Peter Reason and Hilary Bradbury Eds. Handbook of Action Research, Sage, pp 59-66.

McMunn, A., Nazroo, J., Wahrendorf, M., Breeze, E. & Zaninotto, P. (2009). Participation in socially-productive activities, reciprocity and well-being in later life: baseline results in England. Ageing & Society, 29. pp. 765–782.

Mental Health Foundation (2010). Mindfulness Report, p. 6. London. Sited by Chaskalson, M. (2011). The Mindful Workplace – Developing Resilient Individuals and Resonant Organizations with MBSR. p. 3. John Wiley and Sons, Ltd. UK.

Monster (2015). Monster Jobs – Job Search, Career Advice and Hiring Resources. Available at https://www.monster.co.uk/ (Accessed 25/10/16).

Moore, T. (2017). Ageless Soul. Simon and Schuster UK Ltd. London.

Moore, T. (2017). Soulful Ageing. Available at www.SpiritualityandPractice. com (Accessed 11/07/17).Nimrod, G. (2008). In support of innovation theory: innovation in activity patterns and life satisfaction among recently retired individuals. Ageing & Society, 28 pp. 831–846. Ogunbameru, O.A. & Asa, S (2008). Transition to retirement: effect of participation in preretirement education in Nigeria. Educational Gerontology, 34(5) pp. 418–427.

Osborne, J. W (2012). Psychological Effects of the Transition to Retirement. Canadian Journal of Counselling and Psychotherapy. Vol. 46 No 1. pp 45–58.

Parry, J. & Taylor, R. (2007) Orientation, opportunity and autonomy: why people work after state pension age in three areas of England. Ageing & Society, 27 pp. 579–598.

Pension Act (1995). Available at www.lesiglation.goc.uk/ukpga/1995/26/ contents/enacted (Accessed 02/05/17)

Pension Act (2007). Available at www.dwp.gov.uk/policy/pensions-re-form/the pensions-act-2007/ (Accessed 15/03 17)

Pepin, G., & Deutscher, B (2011). "The lived experience of Australian retir-ees: "I'm retired, what do I do now?"British Journal of Occupational Therapy. 74(9) pp 419–426.

Pettican, A. & Prior, S. (2011). "It's a new way of life": an exploration of the occupational transition of retirement. British Journal of Occupational Therapy. 74 (1) 12–19.

Phillipson, C. & Baars, J. (2007). Social Theory and Social Ageing.I n: Bond, J., Peace, S., Dittman-Kohli, F. & Westerhof, G. (eds) Ageing in Society. London: Sage, pp. 68–84 .

Pienta, A.M. (2003). Partners in marriage: An analysis of husbands' and wives' retirement behavior. Journal of Applied Gerontology, 22(3) pp. 340–358.

Pollard, N. (2006). The baby boom: coming of age? British Journal of Occupational Therapy, 69(6), p. 247.

Price, C.A. & Balaswamy, S. (2009). Beyond health and wealth: Predictors of women's retirement satisfaction. International Journal of Aging & Human Development, 68(3) pp. 195–214.

Pushkar, D., Chaikelson, J., Conway, M., Etezadi, J., Giannopoulus, C., Li, K. & Wrosch, C. (2010). Testing Continuity and Activity Variables as Predictors of Positive and Negative Affect in Retirement. Journal of Gerontology: Psychological Sciences. 65B(1) pp. 42–49.

Reed, J., Stanley, D. & Clarke, C. (2004). Health, well-being and older people. Bristol: Policy Press.

Reynolds, F. (2009). Taking up arts & crafts in later life: a qualitative study of the experiential factors that encourage participation in creative activities. British Journal of Occupational Therapy, 71(9), pp. 393–400.

Roberts, G. W. & Machon, A. (2015). Appreciative Healthcare Practice: A guide to compassionate person-centred care. M & K Pub.

Rogers,C. (1983). Freedom to Learn in the 80's. Ohio, Charles Merrill Publishing Co.

Rubin, R, Kerrell, R. & Roberts, G, W. (2011). Appreciative inquiry in occupational therapy education. British Journal of Occupational Therapy. 74.(5). 233–240.

Seligman, M,E,P. & Maier,S,F. (1967).Failure to escape traumatic shock. Journal of Experimental Psychology. 74. 1–9.

Seligman,M,E,P. (2002). Authentic Happiness. New York: Free Press.

Seligman, M,E,P. & Csikszentmihalyi,M. (2000). Positive Psychology : An Introduction. American Psychologist, 55 (1), p 5–14.

Seligman, M.E.P. & Maier, S. F. (1967). Failure to escape traumatic shock. Journal of Experimental Psychology, 74, 1–9

Shuey, K.M. (2004) Worker Preferences, Spousal Coordination, and Participation in an Employer-Sponsored Pension Plan. Research on Ageing, 26(3). pp 287–316.

Siegel, D. J. (2007). The Mindful Brain. New York, NY: Norton.

Slay, G., (2007). Let's get spiritual, Mental Health Practice 12 (11 no. 4) 26–28

Wikipedia (2007). The Free Encyclopaedia, Self-Awareness. Available at http://en.wikipedia.org./wiki/Self_Awareness [Accessed 14th March 2017]

Soidre, T. (2005) Retirement-age preferences of women and men aged 55–64 years in Sweden. Ageing & Society, 25. pp. 943–963.

Stewart, A. (2005). Transitions and retirement. British Journal of Occupational Therapy, 68(12), p. 537.

The Mindful Initiative (2014). Mindful Nation UK. Available at www.the-mindfulnessinitiative.org.uk (Accessed 29th May 2017).

Tinker, A. (1997). Older People in Modern Society (fourth edition). London: Longman.

Torp,L. & Sage,S. (2002). Problems as possibilities: PBL for K-16 (2nd Ed). Association of Supervision and Curriculum Development. Alexandria, Virginia.

Townsend, P. (1981). The Structured Dependency of the Elderly: A Creation of Social Policy in the Twentieth Century. Ageing & Society, 1(1) pp. 5–28.

United Nations (1992). United Nations Principles for Older Persons. http://www.un.org/esa/socdev/ageing/un_principles.html [Accessed 27/11.16].

United Nations (2010). Current Status of the Social Situation, Well-being, Participation in Development and Rights of Older Persons Worldwide. United Nations.

Victor, C. (2005). The Social Context of Ageing. London: Routledge.

Welsh Assembly Government (2003). The Strategy for Older People in Wales. Cardiff: Welsh Assembly Government.

Welsh Assembly Government (2006). National Service Framework for Older People in Wales. Cardiff: Welsh Assembly Government.

Welsh Assembly Government (2007). The Strategy for Older People in Wales 2008–2013: Living longer, living better. Cardiff: Welsh Assembly Government.

Wilcock, A. (2001). Occupation for Health, 1: A journey from self help to prescription. London. British Association and College of Occupational Therapists.

Wilcock, A. (1998). An Occupational Perspective on Health. Thorofare, NJ.

Wilson, M. (2009). As Our Parents. Assumptions about being old. https://asourparentsage.net/2009/11/30/assumptions-about-being-old/ (Accessed 18/08/17).

Wong, A. S. L., (2003). Self-awareness. Available at http://vtaide.com/lifeskills/self_awareness.htm [Accessed 08/12/16]

World Health Organisation (2002). Active Ageing: A Policy Framework. Geneva: World Health Organisation.

World Health Organisation (2004). www.who.int/mediacentre/news/releases/2004/pr60/en/print.html [Accessed 19.11.09]

Yerxa, E., Clark, F., Jackson, J., Parham, D., Pierce, D., & Stein, C.. (1998). An introduction to occupational science, A foundation for occupational therapy in the 21st century. Occupational Therapy in Health Care, 6(4), pp 1–17.

BIBLIOGRAPHY

Appadurai, A. (1996). Modernity at Large: Cultural Dimensions of Globalization. Minneapolis: University of Minnesota.

Appadurai, A. (Ed.) (2000). Globalization: Public Culture. Durham, NC: Duke University.

Atchley, R. (1976). The Sociology of Retirement. Cambridge, MA: Schenkman.

Back, K. (1977). The Ambiguity of Retirement. In Busse & P. Pfeiffer (eds), Behavior and Adaptation in Later Life. E. Boston: Little & Brown.

Baldacchino, D., (2003) Spirituality in Illness and Care, Malta: Preca Library

Baptiste, S., (1997) Spiritually speaking. Canadian Journal of Occupational Therapy 64 (3) 104–105.

Beagan, B., & Kumas-Tun, Z., (2005). Witnessing Spirituality in Practice, British Journal of Occupational Therapy. 68 (1). pp 17–24.

Beeson, D. (1975). Women and Aging, A Critique and Suggestion. Social Problems, 23: pp 52–59.

Belcham, C., (2004). Spirituality in Occupational Therapy: Theory in Practice? British Journal of Occupational Therapy. 67 (1). pp 39–46.

Brim, O.G, Jr (1976). Theories of the Male Mid-Life Crisis. Counselling Psychologist. 1976, Vol. 6, p2–9.

Calasanti, T. M., & Zajicek, A. M. (1993). A socialist-feminist approach to aging: Embracing diversity. Journal of Aging Studies, 7, pp 117–131.

Calasanti, T. (1996). Incorporating diversity: Meaning, levels of research, and implications for theory. The Gerontologist, 36, pp 147–157.

Clark, M. (1968). The Anthropology of Aging, A New Area for Culture and Personality Studies. In B. Neugarten (ed), Middle Age and Aging. Chicago: University of Chicago.

Clark, M. (1972). An Anthropological View of Retirement. In F. Carp (ed), Retirement. New York: Behavioral Publications.

Clark, M., & Anderson, B. (1968). Culture and Aging: An Anthropological Study of Older Americans. Springfield, IL: Charles Thomas. Google Scholar

Collins, M., (2007) Spirituality and the Shadow: Reflection and Therapeutic Use of Self, British Journal of Occupational Therapy, 70 (2). pp 88–90.

Cooperrider, D. L. (1986). Appreciative Inquiry: Towards a methodology for understanding and enhancing organisational innovation. Unpublished PhD. diss., Case Western Reserve University, Cleveland OH.

Cooperrider, D.L. (1999). Positive image, positive action. The affirmative basis of organising in Srivastva, S. and Cooperider, D. L. (Eds.). Appreciative management and leadership: the power of positive thought and action in organisations, rev. ed. (pp. 91–125). Cleveland OH: Lakeshore Communications.

Corlett,E.S & Milner,N.B (1993) .Navigating Mid-Life: Using Typology as a Guide. California: Consulting Psychologist Press Book.

Cornelius,N (ed) (2002). Building Workplace Equality: Ethics, Diversity and Inclusion. London: Thomson.

Crist, P,H. Davis,C.G,& Coffin,P.S. (2000). The effects of employment and mental health status on the balance of work, play/leisure, self care and rest. Occupational Therapy in Mental Health, 15 (1) p 27–42.

Counts, D. (1991). Aging, Health, and Women in West New Britain. Journal of Cross-Cultural Gerontology. 6: pp 277–285.

Cowgill, D. &. H. L. (1972). Aging and Modernization. New York: Appleton-Century-Crofts.

Donahue, W., Orbach, H., & Pollack, O. (1960). Retirement: The Emerging Social Pattern. In C. Tibbitts (ed), The Handbook of Social Gerontology. Chicago, IL: University of Chicago.

Fairhurst, E. (2003) New Identities in Ageing: Perspectives on Age, Gender and Life After Work. In: Arber, S., Davidson, K. & Ginn, J. (eds) Gender and Ageing: Changing Roles and Relationships, pp. 31–46

Foner, A., & Kertzer, D. (1978). Transitions Over the Life Course: Lessons From Age Set Societies. American Journal of Sociology, 83(5): pp 1081–1104.

Fortes, M. (1987). The Concept of the Person Among the Tallensi. In M. Fortes and J. Goody (eds.), Religion, Morality and the Person. Cambridge: Cambridge University.

Fortes, M. (1984). Age, Generation and Social Structure. In D. Ketzer and J. Keith (eds), Age and Anthropological Theory. Ithaca, NY: Cornell University.

Fortes, M. (1958). Introduction. In J. Goody (ed), The Developmental Cycle of Domestic Groups. Cambridge, MA: Cambridge University.

Friedman, E., & Havighurst, R. (1954). The Meaning of Work and Retirement. Chicago: University of Chicago

Fredrickson, B.L. (1998). What good are positive emotions? Review of General Psychology, 2: pp 300–319.

Fredrickson, B.L. (2003). Positive Emotions and Upward Spirals in Organizations, Chapter 11, in Cameron, K.S., Dutton, J.E. and R.E. Quinn (2003). Positive Organizational Scholarship – foundations of a new discipline, San Francisco: Berrett-Kochler Publishers, Inc.

Geertz, C. (1975). The Nature of Anthropological Understanding. American Scientist, 63: pp 47–53.

Geertz, C. (1966). Religion as a Cultural System. London: Tavistock.

Giles, R. (1949). How to Retire – And Enjoy It. New York: Whittlesey House.

Glascock, F. (1981). Social Asset or Social Burden: An Analysis of the Treatment of the Aged in Non-Industrial Societies. In Christine. Fry (ed.), Dimensions: Aging, Culture and Health. Brooklyn: JF Bergin.

Goody, J. (1976). Aging in Non-Industrial Societies. In R. Binstock and E. Shanas (eds), The Handbook of Aging and the Social Sciences. NY: Van Nostrand Rheinhold.

Gordon, M. (1981). Old Age and Loss of Household Headship: A National Irish Study. Journal of Marriage and Family 43 (3): pp 741–747.

Gould,R (1978). Transformations in Mid – Life. 1979, Vol. 10, part 2, p 2–9.

Graebner, W. (1980). A History of Retirement: The Meaning and Function of an American Institution: 1885–1978. New Haven: Yale University Press.

Guillemard, A–M. (1991). International Perspectives on Early Withdrawl from the Labor Force. In J. Miles and J. Quadagno (eds), States, Labor Markets and the Future of Old-Age Policy. Philadelphia: Temple University Press.

Holmberg, A. (1961). Age in the Andes. In R. Kleemier (ed), Aging and Leisure. New York: Oxford University.

Holmes, L. (1976). Trends in Anthropological Gerontology. International Journal of Aging and Human Development. 7(30): pp 220–221.

Hunter,S. & Sundel, M. (Eds) (1989). Midlife Myths: Issues, Findings and Practice Implications. London: Sage Publications.

LeDoux, J.E. (2002). Emotion, Memory, and the Brain. Scientific American, 12: pp 62–71.

Jacobsen, D. (1974). The Rejection of the Retiree Role: A Study of Female Industrial Workers in their 50s. Human Relations. 27(5): pp 477–492.

Jaslow, P. (1976). Employment, Retirement and Morale Among Older Workers. Journal of Gerontology. 31(2): pp 212–218.

Katz, S. (1996). Disciplining Old Age: The Formation of Gerontological Knowledge. Charlottesville, VA: University Press of Virginia.

Kaustenbaum,R. (1992). The Creative Process: A Life-Span Approach. In: Cole, T.R. Van Tassel, D.D, and Katenaum,R (Eds). Handbook of the Humanities and Aging. New York: Springer Publishing Company.

Kets de Vries ,M.F.R (1978). The Midcareer Conundrum. Organizational Dynamics. 1978, Vol. 7, p 45–62.

Keyes, C.L.M & Ryff, C.D (1999). Psychological Well-Being in Midlife. In: Willis, S.L and Reid, J.D (1999). (Eds) Life in the Midlife: Psychological and Social Development in Middle Age. London: Academic Press.

Kielselbach, T (1988). Youth unemployment and health effects. The International Journal of Social Psychiatry, 34.(2). p 83–96.

Kreps, J. (1977) Economics of Retirement. In E. Busse & E. Pfeiffer (eds), Behavior and Adaptation in Later Life. Boston: Little, Brown & Co.

Lindridge, A., (2007) Spirituality Matters, Mental Health Today (12). p 30–33

Luborsky, M. (1994). The Retirement Process: Making the Person and Cultural Meanings Malleable. Medical Anthropology Quart. 8 (4): pp 411–29.

Maddox, L. (1966). Retirement As a Social Event in the U.S. In B. Neugarten (ed), Middle Age and Aging. Chicago: University of Chicago.

Mc Adams ,D.P (1993). The Stories We Live By: Personal Myths and the Making of the Self. New York: William Morrow and Company Inc.

Moen ,P. & Wethington ,E. (1999). Midlife Development in a Life Course Context. In: Willis, S.L and Reid,J.D (1999) (Eds) Life in the Middle: Psychological and Social Development in Middle Age. London: Academic Press.

Oles,P.K (1999). Towards a Psychological Model of the Midlife Crisis. Psychological Reports. 1999. Vol 84 (3,Pt2) June 1999. p 1059–1069.

Palmore, E. (1977). Why Do People Retire? International Journal of Aging and Human Development. 2: pp 269–283.

Palmore, E., & Maddox, L. (1977). Sociological Aspects of Aging. In E. Busse, & E. Pfeiffer (eds), Behavior and Adaptation in Late Life. Boston: Little, Brown & Co.

Powell, A., (2005) Spirituality, healing and the mind, Spirituality and Health International 6 (3): pp 166–172.

Quadagno, J. (1982). Aging in Early Industrial Society: Work, Family and Social Policy in Nineteenth Century England. NY: Academic.

Quadagno, J. S., & Fobes, C. (1995). The welfare state and the cultural reproduction of gender. Social Problems, 42, pp 171–190.

Reid, J.D & Willis, S. L. (1999) . Middle Age: New Thoughts, New Directions. In: Willis, S.L and Reid, J.D. (1999) (Eds). Life in the Middle: Psychological and Social Development in Middle Age. London: Academic Press.

Reynolds, F. (2009) Taking up arts and crafts in later life: a qualitative study of the experiential factors that encourage participation in creative activities. British Journal of Occupational Therapy, 71(9), pp. 393–400

Rhee, D. (1974). Human Aging and Retirement. General Secretariat International Social Security Association. NY: WHO.

Riley, M. (1988). Sociological Lives. Newbury Park, CA: Sage.

Rogers, C. (1961). On Becoming a Person. Boston: Houghton Mifflin.

Rosenberg, S.D., Rosenberg,H.J & Farrell,M.P. (1999). The Midlife Crisis Revisited. In: Willis, S.L and Reid, J.D. (1999) (Eds). Life in the Middle: Psychological and Social Development in Middle Age. London: Academic Press.

Ross, J. (1977). Old People, New Lives: Community Creation in Retirement. Chicago: University of Chicago.

Rustom, C. (1961). The Later Years of Life and the Use of Time Among the Burmans. In R. Kleemier (ed), Aging and Leisure. New York: Oxford.

Sangree, W. (1966). Age, Prayer and Politics in Tiriki, Kenya. NY: Oxford.

Sargent, S. (1977). Coping with Unwanted Variables in Cross Cultural Research: Examples from Mental Health and Treatment of Aging. In L. Adler (ed), Issues in Cross Cultural Research. New York: New York Academy of Sciences.

Savishinsky, J. (2000). Breaking the Watch: The Meanings of Retirement in America. Ithaca: Cornell University.

Shanas, E. (1972). Adjustment to Retirement. In. F. Carp (ed), Retirement. New York: Behavioral Publications.

Seligman, M.E.P.; & Csikszentmihalyi, M. (2000). Positive Psychology: An Introduction. American Psychologist 55 (1): pp 5–14.

Seligman, M.E.P. (2002). Authentic Happiness. New York: Free Press

Simmons, L. (1945). The Role of the Aged in Primitive Societies. London: Yale.

Smith, B (1996). Working Choices.In Hales,G. (eds). Beyond Disability, Towards Enabling Society. Sage: London.

Southorn, R. (2000). Talent down the drain. Open Mind, (106). p 16–17.

Stein, M. (1983). In the Middle. Dallas Texas: Spring Publications.

Stevens,A (1990) . Erik Erikson. Milton Keynes: The Open University Press.

Stanley, S. (1954). The need for positive regard: A contribution to client-centered theory. Unpublished PhD. thesis, University of Chicago. 1954

Sumsion, T., (2006) Overview of client-centred practice. In T. Sumsion (ed.) Client-centred Practice in Occupational Therapy: A Guide to Implementation, USA: Churchill Livingstone Elsevier pp 1–18

Swindon, J., (2006) Spirituality and Mental Health Care: Rediscovering a 'forgotten' dimension, London: Jessica Kingsley Publishers.

Wink, P., & Dillon, M., (2002). Spiritual Development Across the Adult Life Course: Findings From a Longitudinal Study, Journal of Adult Development. 9 (1). pp 79–94.

Wolf, M.A (1991). The Discovery of Middle Age: An Educational Task in Training Gerontologists. Educational Gerontology: 1991. Nov–Dec, Vol 17 (6), p 559–571.

HERZ FÜR AUTOREN A HEART FOR AUTHORS À L'ÉCOUTE DES AUTEURS MIA KAPΔIA ΓIA ΣΥΓ
ARTA FÖR FÖRFATTARE UN CORAZÓN POR LOS AUTORES YAZARLARIMIZA GÖNÜL VERELIM S
HUORE PER AUTORI ET HJERTE FOR FORFATTERE EEN HART VOOR SCHRIJVERS TEMOS OS AU
FÜZO INKÉRT SERCE DLA AUTORÓW EIN HERZ FÜR AUTOREN A HEART FOR AUTHORS À L'ÉCC
RAÇAO ВСЕЙ ДУШОЙ К АВТОРАМ ETT HJÄRTA FÖR FÖRFATTARE Á LA ESCUCHA DE LOS AUT
AUTEURS MIA KAPΔIA ΓIA ΣΥΓΓΡΑΦΕΙΣ UN CUORE PER AUTORI ET HJERTE FOR FORFATTERE EEL
ARLARIMIZA GÖNÜL VERELIM INKÉRT SERCE DLA AUTORÓW EIN HERZ F
VOOR SCHRIJV RS OS BCEЙ ДУШОЙ К АВТОРАМ ETT HJÄRTA F

The authors

Dr Gwilym Wyn Roberts has worked in health and social care practice and education for over 30 years. He gained a Master's degree in Further and Higher Education from the Institute of Education in London and a Professional Doctorate from the School of Social Sciences at Cardiff University. He was Director of Occupational Therapy and Senior Lecturer at Cardiff University until 2016, when he retired from full-time paid employment at the age of 55. He now works as a healthcare educational consultant and a retirement coach.

Robert Workman qualified as an occupational therapist in 2003, graduating from Cardiff University with a first class degree. In 2011 he gained a Masters degree in Ageing Studies from Swansea University. Robert is currently an occupational therapy manager in South Wales. He engages in a variety of meaningful activities and is already planning for his retirement in 20 years' time!

novum PUBLISHER FOR NEW AUTHORS

The publisher

*He who stops
getting better
stops being good.*

This is the motto of novum publishing, and our focus
is on finding new manuscripts, publishing them and
offering long-term support to the authors.
Our publishing house was founded in 1997, and since
then it has become THE expert for new authors and
has won numerous awards.

**Our editorial team will peruse each manuscript
within a few weeks free of charge and without
obligation.**

You will find more information about
novum publishing and our books on the internet:

w w w . n o v u m - p u b l i s h i n g . c o . u k